Nontoxic: Masculinity, Allyship, and Feminist Philosophy

Ben Almassi

# Nontoxic: Masculinity, Allyship, and Feminist Philosophy

Ben Almassi
Govenors State University
University Park, IL, USA

ISBN 978-3-031-13070-0          ISBN 978-3-031-13071-7   (eBook)
https://doi.org/10.1007/978-3-031-13071-7

© The Author(s) 2022. This book is an open access publication.

**Open Access**  This book is licensed under the terms of the Creative Commons Attribution 4.0 International License (http://creativecommons.org/licenses/by/4.0/), which permits use, sharing, adaptation, distribution and reproduction in any medium or format, as long as you give appropriate credit to the original author(s) and the source, provide a link to the Creative Commons licence and indicate if changes were made.

The images or other third party material in this book are included in the book's Creative Commons licence, unless indicated otherwise in a credit line to the material. If material is not included in the book's Creative Commons licence and your intended use is not permitted by statutory regulation or exceeds the permitted use, you will need to obtain permission directly from the copyright holder.

The use of general descriptive names, registered names, trademarks, service marks, etc. in this publication does not imply, even in the absence of a specific statement, that such names are exempt from the relevant protective laws and regulations and therefore free for general use.

The publisher, the authors, and the editors are safe to assume that the advice and information in this book are believed to be true and accurate at the date of publication. Neither the publisher nor the authors or the editors give a warranty, expressed or implied, with respect to the material contained herein or for any errors or omissions that may have been made. The publisher remains neutral with regard to jurisdictional claims in published maps and institutional affiliations.

Pattern © Melisa Hasan

This Palgrave Macmillan imprint is published by the registered company Springer Nature Switzerland AG.
The registered company address is: Gewerbestrasse 11, 6330 Cham, Switzerland

# Acknowledgments

This book was written in Chicago, on the traditional homelands of the Council of Three Fires: the Ojibwe, Odawa, and Potawatomi nations. Many other tribes such as the Ho-Chunk, Fox, Sac, Miami, and Menominee also call these lands home. Located at the confluences of the Chicago and Des Plaines rivers and on Lake Michigan, this region has long been a place for Indigenous people to gather, trade, and maintain kinship ties. Chicago today is home to one of the largest urban American Indian communities in the United States, and the members of this community continue to contribute to the life of the city and celebrate their heritage, practice their traditions, and care for the land and waterways. For more information on the American Indian community in Chicago, visit the American Indian Center (www.aicchicago.org).

Much of the work for this book was done during a sabbatical leave and a course release from my home academic institution, Governors State University (GSU), from 2020 to 2022 as the coronavirus pandemic ravaged the United States and the rest of the world. Thanks to my division chair Jason Zingsheim for supporting this project and to my colleagues at GSU for their critical feedback and advice throughout its development. Words cannot adequately express my gratitude to the teachers, grocery workers, healthcare professionals, and other essential workers in my community, without whom projects like this one and many more urgent endeavors would not have been possible.

The arguments and ideas presented in these pages have benefited from questions, criticisms, and suggestions from editors, peer referees, conference participants, and many other interlocutors. Earlier versions of these chapters were shared at meetings of the Society for Analytical Feminism, Feminist Epistemologies, Methodologies, Metaphysics, and Science Studies, Northeast Modern Language Association, North American Society for Social Philosophy, and GSU's Gender Matters Conference. My thanks to the organizers, speakers, commentators, and other participants in these events. Chapters 5 and 6 are based in part on my 2015 article "Feminist Reclamations of Normative Masculinity," published in *Feminist Philosophy Quarterly* (*FPQ*). I am grateful to anonymous reviewers for their role in bringing this article to fruition and to *FPQ* editors for granting permission to reuse parts of it here. Thanks also to my editor Amy Invernizzi, her colleagues at Palgrave Macmillan, and the reviewers whose criticisms and recommendations have greatly improved the final version of this book.

I am thankful for the critical feedback on various parts of this project offered by many people including Jonathan Allan, Lisa Day, Nick Doctor, Kristie Dotson, Lars Enden, Jeremy Fischer, Rachel Fredericks, Fran Kostarelos, Becky Munk, Kate Norlock, Chris Partridge, Nick Partridge, Brad Smith, Mana Tahaie, and Christopher White. Thanks most of all go to my parents Jenny and Phil Partridge, my partner in all things Negin Almassi, and our wonderful little emerald Zeydi. If the family can be a school of despotism, as Harriet Taylor and John Stuart Mill trenchantly warned, I am so very grateful that ours has been one of love and support.

# Contents

| | | |
|---|---|---|
| 1 | **Introduction** | 1 |
| | *Alternatives to Toxicity* | 1 |
| | *What's to Come* | 4 |
| | *Guiding Priorities* | 8 |
| | *References* | 10 |
| 2 | **Masculinity in Early Feminist Philosophy** | 15 |
| | *Vindications of Masculinity* | 16 |
| | *Much Thought and Much Feeling* | 20 |
| | *Human Virtues, Gendered Roles* | 23 |
| | *Alternative Masculinities and Feminist Androgynies* | 25 |
| | *References* | 27 |
| 3 | **Androgyny and the End of Manhood** | 31 |
| | *Prison Break* | 31 |
| | *I Am (Refusing to Be) a Man* | 33 |
| | *A Gender Reset?* | 36 |
| | *Trouble with Double Vision* | 38 |
| | *References* | 40 |
| 4 | **Feminist Reclamations of Masculinity** | 43 |
| | *Envisioning Feminist Masculinity* | 44 |
| | *Real Men and Just Guys* | 47 |

|   |   |   |
|---|---|---|
| | *Making Masculinity Meaningful* | 50 |
| | *Mindful (of) Masculinity* | 54 |
| | *References* | 57 |
| 5 | **Allyship and Feminist Masculinity** | 61 |
| | *The Whiteness Problem* | 61 |
| | *Feminist Allyship: A Relational Account* | 63 |
| | *Ally Trouble?* | 70 |
| | *Allyship and Intersectionality* | 75 |
| | *References* | 77 |
| 6 | **Allyship Masculinities in the Unjust Meantime** | 83 |
| | *Deeply Nonideal Masculinity* | 84 |
| | *Intersectionality Revisited* | 85 |
| | *What Men Can Know* | 88 |
| | *Putting Privilege to Work* | 93 |
| | *Relational Allyship and Accountability* | 101 |
| | *References* | 103 |
| 7 | **Afterword: Man Up/Stand Up** | 109 |
| | *References* | 111 |

Index                                                                                    113

# About the Author

**Ben Almassi** is Professor of Philosophy and Affiliated Faculty in Gender and Sexuality Studies, Interdisciplinary Studies, and Political and Social Justice Studies at Governors State University on the far Southside of Chicago. He is the author of *Reparative Environmental Justice in a World of Wounds* (2020) and numerous articles in peer-reviewed journals and collections including "Relationally Responsive Expert Trustworthiness" in *Social Epistemology* (2022), "Beyond Science Wars Redux: Feminist Philosophy of Science as Trustworthy Science Criticism" in *Hypatia* (2019), "Epistemic Injustice and its Amelioration" in *Social Philosophy Today* (2018), and "Toxic Funding" in *Journal of Applied Philosophy* (2016). He holds his doctorate from the University of Washington, 2009, and taught at the College of Lake County before joining the faculty at GSU in 2013. When not in the classroom, Ben can be found with his family tramping in forests, wetlands, dunes, and tallgrass prairies throughout the Chicago wilderness.

CHAPTER 1

# Introduction

**Abstract** This chapter introduces the concept of toxic masculinity—as a useful hermeneutical resource, an object of critical scrutiny, and a reminder of the need for alternative normative visions for what men and masculinity should be. It also identifies the major theoretical and methodological priorities guiding my approach throughout this book in evaluating existing visions for alternatives to toxic masculinity and making the case for allyship masculinity as one such alternative not only compatible with but grounded in feminist values and practices.

**Keywords** Conceptual change • Feminist philosophy • Toxic masculinity

## Alternatives to Toxicity

Toxic masculinity is no good for anyone, but the *concept* of toxic masculinity can be quite useful. Sometimes a new idea is developed, or an old idea is reworked in a new way, and with it we find ourselves better able to understand some meaningful part of the world and how we experience it. In this way we strengthen our hermeneutical resources. The concept of spacetime was like this for our understanding of relativistic physics in the early twentieth century (Fine 1978, 333); the concept of sexual harassment was like this for our understanding of sexual discrimination and oppression in the late twentieth century (Fricker 2007, 149); the concept

© The Author(s) 2022
B. Almassi, *Nontoxic: Masculinity, Allyship, and Feminist Philosophy*,
https://doi.org/10.1007/978-3-031-13071-7_1

of climate legacy may play a similar role for our understanding of climate change and intergenerational justice in the twenty-first century (Fredericks 2021).

What then is especially illuminating about the idea of toxic masculinity? In part it is the layered connotations of toxicity: not just that masculinity is bad, but more than this, that *this* masculinity in question is bad *for* men *and* those around them. Toxic masculinity poisons us. We do not have to be reminded that it is harmful for men as well as women and other people: that is baked into the concept. Nor is the central message that masculinity is actually bad for men *rather than* for women, some apparent refutation of core feminist principles. Toxic masculinity hurts everyone it touches (Marcotte 2017; Sculos 2017).

Another thing this idea captures is that men themselves need not be inherently toxic even as the toxicity is closely linked to *how* men are men. "The term thus does not mean that there is something fundamentally wrong about being male," Michael Flood (2018) explains. "But there is something fundamentally wrong with some particular versions of how to be a man." As Terry Kupers puts it in "Toxic Masculinity as a Barrier to Mental Health Treatment in Prison," among the first scholarly uses of the concept, "Toxic masculinity is the constellation of socially regressive male traits that serve to foster domination, the devaluation of women, homophobia, and wanton violence" (2005, 714). On the one hand we have the hopeful suggestion that the problem is not men but rather how we perform masculinity. On the other hand this hopeful suggestion raises a challenging (although not necessarily hopeless) follow-up question, what makes us men if not for our masculinity?

Contrary to conservative critics' reading of the concept of toxic masculinity as an attack on manhood itself, Kupers does not take masculinity to be entirely, irredeemably toxic (Kupers 2005; Salter 2019). As Sam de Boise (2019) observes, "the term 'toxic masculinity' potentially increases receptivity to the notion that there are harmful and non-harmful forms of masculinity, as well as operating as an analytic tool allowing masculinity scholars to talk in normative terms of what masculinity *should* be rather than simply describing what it appears to be." Like rainy days, rotten fruit, and blood diamonds, the grammatical structure itself invites (though does not guarantee) the inference that there are other, better kinds of masculinity to be had. "Toxic masculinity" draws our attention to its poisonous manifestations in ourselves and in others and calls us to find something nontoxic instead.

Just as toxic masculinity invites critical scrutiny, the concept of toxic masculinity is not without its critics either. One concern raised is that the language of toxicity positions men as victims who are passively infected, rather than highlighting their agency in actively reproducing masculinity (Waling 2019, 368). Here I think that those who find the concept of toxic masculinity useful should take the criticism, and gratefully so. Whatever else it is, we should recognize toxic masculinity as something men individually and collectively participate in—not inevitably, but not just passively either. If toxic masculinity is a putrid smog, it is something we create as much as something we take in. A related concern is that talk of toxic masculinity individualizes what should be theorized in social structural terms (de Boise 2019). One way to put this is that "treating sexism as a character flaw of *some* men" (Harrington 2021) thus neatly isolates responsibility for gender inequities and injustices to a subset of clearly bad men—not *us*, of course. It also potentially obscures a crucial insight of Connell and Messerschmidt's (2005) characterization of masculinities as *configurations of practices*, not just individual attitudes or expectations. Here again I share these critics' concerns, even if I am more optimistic that our understanding of toxic masculinity can and should include a structural analysis rather than reducing it to the deviant behaviors of a few safely ostracized men. Furthermore, as Salter (2019) warns, people who oppose toxic masculinity must resist seeing it in universal or ahistorical terms: we cannot assume that "the causes of male violence and other social problems are the same everywhere, and therefore, that the solutions are the same as well."

Another criticism of the concept of toxic masculinity builds on the aforementioned idea that its formulation suggests the potential for—but does not much specify the substance of—a contrasting nontoxic counterpart. "It is quite clear what we mean by a 'toxic masculinity,'" Andrea Waling (2019, 368) writes; "there is less consensus as to what we might mean by a 'healthy masculinity' despite more pressing needs to encourage it amongst men and boys." What does healthy, nontoxic masculinity look like? Waling is quite right to see little agreement on the matter, and right as well that the concept of toxic masculinity does not answer the question for us. The popular and scholarly literatures are filled not only with diagnoses of the trouble with men today, but also prescriptions of what men can—and should—be instead. These normative visions take many forms. For some it is loving or mindful masculinity (hooks 2004a; Plank 2019); for others, wild manhood and heroic virtue (Bly 1990; Keen 1992). For still others, the desire to separate some sort of healthy manhood from toxic masculinity is itself a mistake—better to refuse to be a man entirely and salvage one's nongendered humanity instead (Stoltenberg 2013; Cooper 2018). Perhaps any claim to masculinity is inevitably a *cruel optimism*, "cruel precisely because we believe and we continue to believe that it is attainable even though we continually fail" (Allan 2018, 182). If not masculinity itself, perhaps worthwhile traits or virtues traditionally associated with masculinity can still be incorporated into an ideal of androgyny (Warren 1982; Sterba 1996). For those suspicious of traditional gender roles and acutely aware of how toxic masculinity can harm people across gender identities, androgyny can present an attractive alternative.

If there *is* nontoxic masculinity to be had, perhaps we can find it in feminist values and practices. At first the very idea of feminist masculinity might seem like a contradiction in terms, something akin to a square circle or George Carlin's old jokes about jumbo shrimp and military intelligence. "Doesn't one negate the other?" the skeptic asks. On this reading we can be feminist or masculine but not both. Maybe it's more like what Gandhi apocryphally said when asked what he thought of Western civilization—that it would be a good idea (Shapiro 2006, 299). My own view is that we can indeed make sense of feminist masculinity, not just hypothetically but in actual practice, such that men as men have distinctive and constructive contributions to make to feminism. In feminist allyship we can find an open-ended model for *ways of being men*, of masculinities predicated on recognizing and actively responding to rather than passively accepting or ignoring the diverse array of privileges, expectations, and experiences that are distinctive of men under patriarchy.

## What's to Come

There is much more to be said about all of this, of course. But for now, in the rest of this chapter, let me begin by outlining the philosophical investigation of masculinity to come and making plain the theoretical and methodological priorities that will guide us along the way.

In Chap. 2 we go back to the origins of Western feminist political philosophy, with particular attention to Mary Wollstonecraft, Harriet Taylor, and John Stuart Mill, to see what sort of critical and constructive visions for men and masculinity we can find there. In the years since publication of Wollstonecraft's *A Vindication of the Rights of Woman* (1792), Taylor's "The Enfranchisement of Women" (1851), and Mill's *The Subjection of*

*Women* (1869), liberal political philosophy has been a fertile ground for feminism. These texts in particular offer powerful criticisms of traditional constructions of femininity and masculinity under systems of sexual inequality, as well as positive visions for women and men as part of their distinctive defenses of sexual equality. The harmful effects of patriarchy on the moral and intellectual characters of both women and men are central to their liberal-feminist analyses. Wollstonecraft's diagnosis is insufficiently rational masculinity all around, and her recommendation is the social promotion and personal development of rational thinking, bodily vigor, and independence for men as well as women, boys as well as girls. Taylor and Mill meanwhile also value rationality but seek to complement it with emotional development, and more generally promote overall human excellence for women and men through reunification of good human properties that have been artificially divided into masculine and feminine. These two feminist responses to patriarchy are not logically exhaustive, but between them, presage many of the scholarly and popular alternatives to toxic masculinity still proposed today.

From here we move on to Chap. 3 to consider the appeal and limitations of feminist androgyny (Warren 1982) as a viable alternative to masculinity and John Stoltenberg's (1989, 1993) emphatic repudiation of manhood and masculinity on radical feminist grounds. We trace how feminist ideals of androgyny and rejections of masculinity recur in one form or another throughout many popular and scholarly accounts of men and manhood. Androgyny need not make us anatomically, socially, or psychologically identical of course, nor will it necessarily license all ungendered human actions. The idea is that femininity and masculinity lose meaning as socially loaded categories; genital and genetic sex differences would become no more socially significant than are height or eye color and social roles, divisions of labor, and personalities would not be indexed to presumed sex differences. Mary Anne Warren and James Sterba are each sympathetic to a sort of feminist moral androgyny, where so-called masculine and feminine virtues are distributed and exhibited among human beings regardless of gender. Stoltenberg meanwhile advocates what he describes as a "double vision" for men of conscience: to be mindful of the present reality of our place as men in a sex-class system while also recognizing "the truth of the possibility of a future without it" (1989, 197).

If we must choose between feminism and masculinity, many men will pick the latter. And yet the resistance to discarding manhood and masculinity comes not only from conservative men and mythopoetic men, but also from writers such as bell hooks and Michael Kimmel who attempt to reclaim masculinity as not only compatible with but grounded in feminist commitments. In Chap. 4 we turn then to feminist reclamations of masculinity. In *We Real Cool* (2004b) and *The Will to Change* (2004a), among other texts, hooks envisions feminist masculinity as a positive alternative to patriarchal masculinity. In *Manhood in America* (1996), Kimmel offers democratic manhood in contrast to traditional masculinity and androgyny; in *Guyland* (2008) he urges young men to move away from immature, unjust masculinity to a deeper masculinity of just guys. There is much to admire in these and other attempts to reclaim feminist masculinity; much of what they identify as constituting better, more mindful masculinity are indeed good human qualities. As a viable guide for men and their allies, however, these accounts fall short, sometimes converging with androgyny, sometimes reinforcing traditional patriarchal masculinity, at other times obscuring if not denying some people's lived experiences and identities. hooks in particular articulates an evocative vision of loving feminist masculinity, yet a central mystery remains: how can love, courage, or justice be meaningfully constitutive of feminist masculinity without thereby assuming that masculinity is whatever male people are and do?

My goal in Chap. 5 then is to offer a conception of feminist masculinity in terms of *allyship practices*: one that aligns with hooks' vision for loving masculinity as a kind of partnership, does so while capably differentiating it from feminist androgyny and patriarchal masculinity, and avoids the vices of arrogance, passivity, and self-glorification that critics see plaguing ally culture today. Here I find that Linda Alcoff's (2006) work on white anti-racism provides at least two insights that extend fruitfully to the question of feminist masculinity. The first is that socially privileged identity and group membership are not easily avowed; the second is that allyship against oppression itself can be constitutive of anti-racist whiteness, through our sustained contributions to justice and an abiding sense of how such contributions fit into anti-racist white histories and communities. In a similar spirit, I propose that feminist allyship practices can ground and give meaning to nontoxic *ways of being men*. Much like a feminist ideal of androgyny, feminist allyship masculinity seeks to upend masculinity as a received social category, but it diverges from feminist androgyny in emphasizing men's distinctive yet non-essentialist contributions.

Feminist allyship on this account builds upon a simultaneous recognition of difference and commonality, such that allies come together in coalition (Reagon 1983) from different locations to work for a shared end. The relational approach to allyship (Sullivan-Clarke 2020) that I advocate here diverges a bit from allyship as frequently taken up in contemporary sociological and popular discussions, where allies are by definition non-beneficiary participants in social justice movements (Myers 2008) or members of dominant groups working with members of oppressed groups (Brown and Ostrove 2013). A relational approach enables a more flexible and intersectional understanding of allyship; it underlines the importance of accountability and the risks that come with prioritizing self-ascribed or institutionally commodified "ally" labels over reparative and constructive allyship practices.

The difference-in-common dimension of feminist allyship so understood is not an impediment to but a collective resource for collaboration across gender and other social differences. In contrast to both traditional patriarchal masculinity and mythopoetic masculinity, building around feminist allyship makes for a decidedly and deliberately nonideal form of masculinity. It is not rooted in gender essentialist or ahistorical claims about men's true nature; rather, the aftermath of historical and ongoing systems of gender oppression is where allyship masculinity is made meaningful. What feminist allyship enables are critically reflective and substantively feminist ways that men can be—not forever and always, but for what Alison Jaggar (2019) calls "the unjust meantime."

Chapter 6 further explores the intersectional potential and challenges for allyship masculinities in social context, in the unjust meantime. What does it mean for feminist allyship masculinities to be open to all men, not in spite of but because of the diversity of social locations and experiences among us? Can we recognize that men can be targets of intersectional gender oppression without implying that men generally experience gender-based oppression, and without denying that men (individually and collectively, pervasively and systematically) receive gender-based privileges and entitlements? Investigating these questions takes us in both epistemological and ethical directions. The epistemological challenges confronted include issues of active ignorance, epistemic injustice, and situated knowledge. What does it mean to achieve a feminist standpoint (Wylie 2012; Toole 2021)? How can we begin thought from lived experiences different from our own (Harding 1990; Narayan 2003)? And how can epistemic humility—which need not imply epistemic deference—be integrated into relations of accountability between allies? The need for accountability raises not just epistemic but also ethical challenges. We conclude by discussing several potential pitfalls and ethical dilemmas for feminist allyship, including the glass escalator (Williams 1992), the pedestal effect (Messner et al. 2015, 138), and the master's tools (Lorde 1984, 110). Putting male privilege to work toward feminist ends is often like wielding a double-edged sword; it is better still when we work together to beat that sword into ploughshares.

## Guiding Priorities

What we seek in a worthwhile model of masculinity is in large part a function of our intended uses. My own approach is informed by a few principal theoretical and methodological priorities:

*Normativity*. Our model should enable cogent criticism of patriarchal norms of masculinity and also underwrite alternative norms of masculinity grounded in feminist commitments. Following Raewyn Connell's taxonomy, normative conceptions of masculinity involve social configurations and expectations of how men should be (Connell 2005, 70), where these gendered configurations and expectations might be imposed upon us by our communities, institutional structures, and even ourselves. To characterize something as toxic masculinity, after all, is not only to describe but also to evaluate it. Despite their significant differences, each of the alternatives to toxic masculinity discussed in the coming chapters is similar in at least this respect, that they offer answers to the question of how men should be. Sometimes their normative analysis is positive, sometimes it is negative, but even those accounts that actively reject masculinity are not neutral about it. In such cases there is still an evaluation made: that what we ought to do is to repudiate masculinity and refuse to be men.

In focusing on normative masculinity, I certainly do not mean to devalue ethnographic or other empirical studies of men and masculinities but rather to take inspiration from Connell's (2000, 14) observation that while descriptive sociological research has indeed produced fruitful results for masculinity studies, social-scientific methodologies do not exhaust the scope of worthwhile study. I also mean to take up Larry May's (1998, 149) call for philosophical work on masculinity to offer not only criticism but also positive visions of what men can be.

*Differentiation*. Unlike with a feminist ideal of androgyny that would evacuate the category of masculinity, a normative model of feminist masculinity must identify key features that effectively differentiate masculinity from non-masculinity. Such features need not be understood as essential properties, nor as necessary and sufficient conditions, but they cannot be both constitutive of masculinity and indistinguishably applicable to those who are not masculine. All men are born and die, for example, which means that all those who embody masculinity are born and will die. Yet to say that mortality is constitutive of masculinity would fail to identify anything distinctive about it, given that people who are not masculine (however we understand that) of course are born and will die too. (Some might respond that mortality is indeed constitutive of masculinity in the sense that men are more accepting, or aware, or in denial about their mortality than other people are. But to whatever extent these claims hold true, it would not be mortality itself but rather our distinctive attitudes toward it that would differentiate masculinity from non-masculinity so understood.)

Differentiation will prove to be a surprisingly difficult challenge for feminist masculinities as compared to traditional patriarchal masculinity, which presumes and reifies all sorts of essentialist ideas about the duality of men and women that feminists quite reasonably reject. The challenge is to find constitutive properties that are somehow meaningfully feminist and normatively masculine in substance.

To clarify, when I discuss expectations (or obligations or feminist contributions) of men *as* men I mean *in virtue of the fact that* they are men, or *because* they are men. It is just a specification of the reference class as opposed to (say) men's obligations as brothers, or friends, or human beings. By analogy, Joe Biden's responsibilities *as* US President might overlap with but are not identical to his responsibilities as a husband or as an American citizen. In discussing normative masculinity in terms of the social configurations and expectations of how men as men should be, I mean things that apply to them because they are men rather than women or gender non-binary people. The phrasing here is not meant to be a roundabout reference to men born as men, men assigned male at birth, or anything like that.

*Intersectionality and Non-Androcentricity.* Our model should allow for multiple instantiations of feminist masculinity given variations among men across race, class, sexuality, and other such categories of social identity. An intersectional feminist approach to masculinity (Crenshaw 1989; Mutua 2012; Taiwo 2018) should not presume that only those men who are allowed to pursue or interested in meeting white, middle-class, cisgender, or heteronormative expectations can be *real* or *good* men, any more than intersectional feminism should presumptively center the experiences or expectations of straight, white, cisgender middle-class women. For these reasons it will be good to consider a plurality of feminist masculinities and challenge both explicit and tacit ways in which some men's distinct experiences of privilege, oppression, or allyship are taken to stand in for men generally.

Our model also should not treat masculinity as some unmarked norm from which oppositional consequences for women, girls, or femininity then automatically follow. It should not take men's masculinity as the central, default, or most significant case with immediate implications for all other gender categories. Men and boys are not the only people who perform masculinity, after all (Halberstam 1998, 276). Whatever else it does for us, our model should not only accommodate intersectional feminist masculinities but also not rule out intersectional female masculinities and genderqueer masculinities. In the search for viable alternatives to toxic masculinity, we must not erase heterogeneous experiences of masculinity, deny non-binary gender identities, or otherwise recapitulate the very toxicities we mean to remedy and replace.

## REFERENCES

Alcoff, Linda. 2006. *Visible Identities: Race, Gender, and the Self.* Oxford: Oxford University Press.

Allan, Jonathan. 2018. Masculinity as Cruel Optimism. *NORMA: International Journal for Masculinity Studies* 13 (3–4): 175–190.

Bly, Robert. 1990. *Iron John: A Book about Men.* Boston: Addison-Wesley.

Brown, Kendrick, and Joan Ostrove. 2013. What Does it Mean to be an Ally? The Perception of Allies from the Perspective of People of Color. *Journal of Applied Social Psychology* 43 (11): 2211–2222.

Connell, R.W. 2000. *The Men and the Boys.* Berkeley: University of California Press.

———. 2005. *Masculinities.* Cambridge: Polity Press.

Connell, R.W., and James Messerschmidt. 2005. Hegemonic Masculinity: Rethinking the Concept. *Gender and Society* 19 (6): 829–859.

Cooper, Wilbert. 2018. All Masculinity is Toxic. *Vice*, July 26.

Crenshaw, Kimberle. 1989. Demarginalizing the Intersection of Race and Sex. *University of Chicago Law Forum* 139.

De Boise, Sam. 2019. Is Masculinity Toxic? *NORMA: International Journal for Masculinity Studies* 14 (3): 147–151.

Fine, Arthur. 1978. Conceptual Change in Mathematics and Science. *PSA: Proceedings of the Biennial Meeting of the Philosophy of Science Association* 1978 (2): 328–341.

Flood, Michael. 2018. Toxic Masculinity: A Primer and Commentary. *XY*, July 7.

Fredericks, Rachel. 2021. Climate Legacy: A Newish Concept for the Climate Crisis. *Environmental Ethics* (Online First).
Fricker, Miranda. 2007. *Epistemic Injustice: Power and the Ethics of Knowing.* Oxford: Oxford University Press.
Halberstam, Jack. 1998. *Female Masculinity.* Durham: Duke University Press.
Harding, Sandra. 1990. Starting Thought from Women's Lives: Eight Resources for Maximizing Objectivity. *Journal of Social Philosophy* 21 (2–3): 140–149.
Harrington, Carol. 2021. What Is 'Toxic Masculinity' and Why Does it Matter? *Men and Masculinities* 24 (2): 345–352.
hooks, bell. 2004a. *The Will to Change: Men, Masculinity, and Love.* New York: Atria Books.
———. 2004b. *We Real Cool: Black Men and Masculinity.* New York: Atria Books.
Jaggar, Alison. 2019. Thinking about Justice in the Unjust Meantime. *Feminist Philosophy Quarterly* 5 (2).
Keen, Sam. 1992. *Fire in the Belly: On Being a Man.* New York: Bantam Books.
Kimmel, Michael. 1996. *Manhood in America: A Cultural History.* New York: The Free Press.
———. 2008. *Guyland.* New York: HarperCollins.
Kupers, Terry. 2005. Toxic Masculinity as a Barrier to Mental Health Treatment in Prison. *Journal of Clinical Psychology* 61 (6): 713–724.
Lorde, Audre. (1984) 2007. *Sister Outsider: Essays and Speeches.* Berkeley: Crossing Press.
Marcotte, Amanda. 2017. Toxic Masculinity is Killing Us in Many Ways. *AlterNet*, October 24.
May, Larry. 1998. *Masculinity and Morality.* Ithaca: Cornell University Press.
Messner, Michael, Max Greenberg, and Tal Peretz. 2015. *Some Men: Feminist Allies and the Movement to End Violence against Women.* Oxford University Press.
Mill, John Stuart. 1869. *The Subjection of Women.* Reprinted in *The Collected Works of John Stuart Mill*, ed. John M. Robson (Toronto: Toronto University Press, 1984), 259–348.
Mutua, Athena D. 2012. Multidimensionality is to Masculinities What Intersectionality is to Feminism. *Nevada Law Journal* 13: 341–367.
Myers, Daniel J. 2008. Ally Identity: The Politically Gay. In *Identity Work in Social Movements*, ed. Jo Reger, Daniel J. Myers, and Rachel L. Einwohner, 167–187. Minneapolis: University of Minnesota Press.
Narayan, Uma. 2003. The Project of Feminist Epistemology: Perspectives from a Non-Western Feminist. In *Feminist Theory Reader*, ed. Carole McCann and Seung-Kyung Kim, 308–317. New York: Routledge.
Plank, Liz. 2019. *For the Love of Men: A New Vision for Mindful Masculinity.* New York: St. Martin's Press.

Reagon, Bernice Johnson. 1983. Coalition Politics: Turning the Century. In *Home Girls: A Black Feminist Anthology*, ed. Barbara Smith. New York: Kitchen Table Press.

Salter, Michael. 2019. The Problem with a Fight against Toxic Masculinity. *The Atlantic*, February 27.

Sculos, Bryant W. 2017. Who's Afraid of 'Toxic Masculinity'? *Class, Race, and Corporate Power* 5 (3): 1–5.

Shapiro, Fred R. 2006. *The Yale Book of Quotations*. New Haven: Yale University Press.

Sterba, James. 1996. Feminist Justice and Sexual Harassment. *Journal of Social Philosophy* 27 (1): 103–122.

Stoltenberg, John. 1989. *Refusing to be a Man: Essays on Sex and Justice*. London: University College London Press.

———. 1993. *The End of Manhood: A Book for Men of Conscience*. London: Dutton.

———. 2013. Why Talking about 'Healthy Masculinity' is like Talking about 'Healthy Cancer'. *Feminist Current*, August 9.

Sullivan-Clarke, Andrea. 2020. Empowering Relations: An Indigenous Understanding of Allyship in North American. *Journal of World Philosophies* 5: 30–42.

Taiwo, Olufemi. 2018. *The Man Not* and the Dilemmas of Intersectionality. *APA Newsletter on Philosophy and the Black Experience* 17 (2): 6–10.

Taylor, Harriet. 1851. The Enfranchisement of Women. Reprinted in *The Collected Works of John Stuart Mill*, ed. John M. Robson. Toronto: Toronto University Press, 1984: 393–416.

Toole, Briana. 2021. Recent Work in Standpoint Epistemology. *Analysis* 81 (2): 338–350.

Waling, Andrea. 2019. Problematising 'Toxic' and 'Healthy' Masculinity for Addressing Gender Inequalities. *Australian Feminist Studies* 34 (101): 362–375.

Warren, Mary Anne. 1982. Is Androgyny the Answer to Sexual Stereotyping? In *'Masculinity,' 'Femininity,' and 'Androgyny': A Modern Philosophical Discussion*, ed. Mary Vetterling-Braggin, 170–185. Totowa, NJ: Rowman & Allanheld.

Williams, Christine. 1992. The Glass Escalator: Hidden Advantages for Men in the 'Female' Professions. *Social Problems* 39: 253–267.

Wollstonecraft, Mary. 1792. *A Vindication of the Rights of Woman*. London: Joseph Johnson.

Wylie, Alison. 2012. Feminist Philosophy of Science: Standpoint Matters. *Proceedings and Addresses of the American Philosophical Association* 86 (2): 47–76.

**Open Access** This chapter is licensed under the terms of the Creative Commons Attribution 4.0 International License (http://creativecommons.org/licenses/by/4.0/), which permits use, sharing, adaptation, distribution and reproduction in any medium or format, as long as you give appropriate credit to the original author(s) and the source, provide a link to the Creative Commons licence and indicate if changes were made.

The images or other third party material in this chapter are included in the chapter's Creative Commons licence, unless indicated otherwise in a credit line to the material. If material is not included in the chapter's Creative Commons licence and your intended use is not permitted by statutory regulation or exceeds the permitted use, you will need to obtain permission directly from the copyright holder.

CHAPTER 2

# Masculinity in Early Feminist Philosophy

**Abstract** In this chapter we turn to early Western feminist political philosophy, with particular attention to Mary Wollstonecraft, Harriet Taylor, and John Stuart Mill, to see what sort of visions for men and masculinity can be found there. Since Wollstonecraft's *Vindication of the Rights of Woman* (1792), Taylor's "The Enfranchisement of Women" (1851), and Mill's *The Subjection of Women* (1869), liberal political philosophy has been a fertile ground for feminism. These texts in particular offer powerful critiques of traditional femininity and distinctive defenses of sexual equality. This is not to say Wollstonecraft, Taylor, and Mill have nothing to say about masculinity or men's relationship to sexual equality; the harmful effects of patriarchy on both women and men are central to their positions. Yet these foundational texts offer limited positive visions for men and masculinity, with a kind of partial androgyny on the one side and universal masculinity on the other.

**Keywords** Liberal feminism • Masculinity • Mill • Political philosophy • Rationality • Wollstonecraft

Victor Frankenstein was an absent father. Those who have read Mary Shelley's *Frankenstein* (1818) know that contrary to old monster movies, Frankenstein was the scientist not the creature. Still I think it is fair to call Frankenstein a monster: as Shelley tells her dark tale, the scientist was just as monstrous as the abominable being that he brought to life. Frankenstein abandons his creature in the very moment of its creation, and indeed denies him and flees from him (fruitlessly, it turns out) to the ends of the earth. Frankenstein's monster is let loose on the world without guidance, care, or education, forced to piece these things together himself while living alone in the shadows.

Mary Shelley has often been called the "mother of science fiction" (Freedman 2002; De Bruin-Mole 2018) as her own mother Mary Wollstonecraft has often been called the "mother of feminism" (Ford 2009; Lewis 2020). Both authors show an acuity for the responsibility that creators have for their creations and the repercussions that follow from them. And as we consider the place of men and masculinity in feminist philosophy, I find it fitting to begin with Wollstonecraft and her great contributions to classic liberalism, *A Vindication of the Rights of Men* (1790) and *A Vindication of the Rights of Woman* (1792). Both texts have specific targets, and yet both have also surpassed these immediate critical tasks in their lasting influences. The first *Vindication* is an ardent defense of liberalism and Enlightenment values against Edmund Burke's (1790) conservative critique of the French Revolution; the second is both a feminist response to and an internal critique of Jean-Jacques Rousseau's philosophy of education in *Emile* (1762). Against Burke, Wollstonecraft goes about dissecting the vagaries, inconsistencies, and essential hollowness of his position, and in the process reiterates the case for natural rights and rationality in liberal social contract theory. Against Rousseau, she argues for the reformation of gender-based education, again reiterating the value of rationality for both women and men.

## Vindications of Masculinity

A common objection to Wollstonecraft's liberal feminism raised by patriarchal contemporaries and later feminist critics is that she aimed to achieve women's equality by turning them into men (Gubar 1994; Bryson 2003, 18). While this does not quite capture her position, it is not too far off. "*Rights of Woman* is preoccupied with championing a kind of masculinity into which women can be invited rather than enlarging or inviting a positive kind of femininity," writes Claudia Johnson (1995, 24). "Wollstonecraft posits rationality, independence, and productive bodily vigor as man's 'true' nature, which culture has perverted into trifling sentimentality, dependence, and weakness." Consider Wollstonecraft's withering criticisms of Burke for his sentimentality and irrationality. "I glow with indignation when I attempt, methodically, to unravel your slavish paradoxes, in which I can find no fixed principles to refute," she writes, in the opening pages of *A Vindication of the Rights of Men*. "I perceive, from the whole tenor of your Reflections, that you have a moral antipathy to reason" (Solomon & Berggren 1983, 242). The essay ends on a similar note: "I pause to recollect myself; and smother the contempt I feel rising for your rhetorical flourishes and infantine sensibility" (263). Indeed, Wollstonecraft is contemptuous throughout of Burke's appeal to sensibility and feeling rather than principle and reason. Of course the cultivation of reason can be difficult, she allows, "and men of lively fancy, finding it easier to follow the impulse of passion, endeavor to persuade themselves and others that it is most *natural*" (251). Burke's conservative defenses of nobility, property, and the clergy are misplaced, she argues—"Man preys on man; and you mourn for the idle tapestry that decorated a Gothic pile, and the dronish bell that summoned a fat priest to prayer" (262)—but even more than that, what bothers Wollstonecraft is that they lack a rational foundation.

In this way, Ruth Abbey explains, Wollstonecraft positions Burke as *unmanly*: "integral to [her] attempt to gender Burke's stands as feminine is her insistence that his attack on the Revolution is irrational" (2019, 7). Abbey continues:

> Indeed, on close inspection, we find that *Vindication of Rights of Men* is populated by a slew of unmanly men. Whole groups suffer from compromised manliness in Wollstonecraft's reckoning although the reasons for, and sources of, their mitigations vary. Rich men, for example, find it hard to achieve independence because so much is done for them and they have no need to struggle…talented people need to endear themselves to the wealthy in order to make their way in the world…Those who are too moral to perform servility will suffer. [2019, 9–10]

Whatever manliness is, we will not find it by taking stock of features shared among existing men. "Manly men are more hypothetical than tautological: in Wollstonecraft's estimation, the condition of manliness is something yet to be achieved on any widespread basis," Abbey (2019, 12) explains. Men's failure to be manly arouses Wollstonecraft's ire for individual men and the social conditions that produce them: "I presume that *rational* men will excuse me for endeavoring to persuade them to become more masculine and respectable" (Solomon & Berggren 1983, 271). This is why moral education is so important. Wollstonecraft believes that "every being may become virtuous by the exercise of its own reason" (274), but this universal potential must be actively developed rather than stifled or perverted by a society's systems of education.

Many traditionalist critics would agree with Wollstonecraft that rationality, independence, and productivity are essential to man's true nature, from which we have disastrously diverged. Where they would disagree, and what makes her argument particularly fascinating, is the claim that these things are—cultural perversions aside—woman's true nature as well. Consider Rousseau, the main target of criticism in *A Vindication of the Rights of Woman*. In contrast to Burke in her earlier essay, Wollstonecraft's critical relationship to Rousseau is more disappointed than antagonistic. The crux of their disagreement is not whether reason is masculine but what Wollstonecraft saw as Rousseau's intellectually inconsistent, anti-Enlightenment assumption that masculine rationality is available to some people (men) but not others (women), as though God had not endowed all of humanity with a capacity for reason. Wollstonecraft writes, "it is a farce to call any being virtuous whose virtues do not result from the exercise of its own reason. This was Rousseau's opinion respecting men: I extend it to women, and confidently assert that they have been drawn out of their sphere by false refinement, and not by an endeavor to acquire masculine qualities" (274–275). To be consistent, Rousseau should either champion or resist the progress of reason in *both* sexes, Wollstonecraft reasons, "for if men eat of the tree of knowledge, women will come in for a taste; but…only attain a knowledge of evil" (273).

Wollstonecraft assures her readers that women's masculinity—masculinity as she advocates it—is not something to be feared but welcomed: "all those who view them with a philosophic eye must, I should think, wish with me that every day they should grow more and more masculine" (269.) Part of the problem, she allows, is that readers might misunderstand her. Wollstonecraft is not suggesting that women join in hunting, shooting, or gaming. She is not encouraging them to abandon their duties as wives and mothers. Indeed, she argues, by cultivating masculinity as she envisions it, women will thus be more capable wives and mothers than they are under conditions of sexual inequality (347).

"Manly is not an adjective attached to a particular set of activities that had been seen as exclusively male," Abbey explains; "any activity can, in principle, be undertaken by any adult in a manly way" (2019, 12). If manliness and masculinity are not about traditionally male activities, gender roles, or male embodiment, what does manliness as Wollstonecraft conceives it actually involve? "On closer inspection, manliness turns out to be a shorthand for the clutch of qualities Wollstonecraft admires," Abbey argues (2019, 12). She continues:

> Ultimately manliness has very little to do with either sex or gender for Wollstonecraft; the term summarizes a set of desirabilia that refer to admirable character traits, egalitarian and meritocratic social and political arrangements and terms of interaction, and the exercise and exchange of talent, effort, and power on just and rational terms. [2019, 15]

For Wollstonecraft the issue is too much sentimentality and not enough rationality, all around, in the education and enculturation of both women and men. Here we might contrast her vision for education with both Rousseau's *Emile*, which warns against educating women like men, but also her contemporary Catharine Macaulay's *Letters on Education* (1790), which as Valerie Bryson notes, goes "beyond uncritical acceptance of male values to demand that the education of boys too be changed to provide them with traditional female skills" (Bryson 2003, 14; see also Boos 1976; Frazer 2011).

In some ways, Wollstonecraft's advocacy of women's liberation through the further cultivation of reason anticipates Simone de Beauvoir's rejection of femininity in *The Second Sex* (1953). As Bryson observes, de Beauvoir "insisted that it is only by overcoming their biology that women can become 'fully human'" (2003, 24). Yet she did not seem to similarly regard either male biology or masculinity as an artificial construction in parallel to femininity that men must likewise overcome in order to achieve their own humanity. If women in patriarchal societies are characteristically and problematically positioned as Other, men's Subject position is not similarly problematized for de Beauvoir's feminist existentialism when it comes to their gender identities.

"The two sexes mutually corrupt and improve each other," Wollstonecraft writes. "This I believe to be an indisputable truth, extending it to every virtue" (Solomon and Berggren 1983, 337). Both men and women have work to do, personally and culturally, in changing our vicious tendencies. As Gal Gerson puts it, "inequality breeds irrationality at *both* ends" (2002, 801). The goal here is not for men and women to meet in the middle, as it were, with women developing traditionally masculine traits and men traditionally feminine ones. For Wollstonecraft, the goal is for both men and women to become more masculine in the sense of becoming more rational, independent, and physically and mentally stronger.

## Much Thought and Much Feeling

In "Mill's Feminism: Liberal, Radical, and Queer," Martha Nussbaum (2010) notices several ways in which modern critics (feminist and otherwise) have failed to give John Stuart Mill a fair reading. His liberal feminism is actually more radical than commentators recognize, Nussbaum argues, not despite but because of its liberalism. Contrary to the idea that liberal feminism cannot address the serious inequalities that women face within marriage and in family structures, because these are "outside" of liberal justice, "Mill carries the traditional liberal critique of feudal and monarchical hierarchies into the sphere of gender relations," Nussbaum says. "He asks liberal thought to be thoroughgoing and consistent, where it has been half-hearted and inconsistent" (2010). Here she rejects the allegation that liberal feminism is insensitive to structural injustice and power dynamics. "Both historically and in today's most influential versions, liberalism is all about undoing hierarchies of power," she explains. "The problem, instead, is the problem that Mill identifies right at the outset of *Subjection*: men who think they are liberals, and in some ways are so, refuse to carry their insights into the domain of gender" (2010). In this way Nussbaum rejects the idea that liberal feminism, as Keith Burgess Jackson (1995, 372) puts it, "accepts the public sphere as it is and seeks to bring women into it on the same terms as men." Where Jackson sees Mill as a radical feminist *rather* than a liberal, Nussbaum sees Mill as radical *because* of his liberal feminism.

The pursuit of equality in the aftermath of patriarchal social and political divisions will certainly require dismantling artificial impediments to women's free and equal participation in public life. But men's experiences and cultivated characteristics will need to change, too. As Nussbaum (2010) notes, "Mill makes at least the beginning of an argument that emotional development, of a sort that many men do not get, is a crucial element of human flourishing." In this way Mill differs from Wollstonecraft, because the problem as he sees it is not limited to the cultivation of reason but the cultivation of sentiment too. For Jackson, his receptivity to femininity is one more thing that makes Mill a radical feminist. "Rather than perpetuate the negativity of these [traditionally feminine coded] characteristics, radical feminism seeks to revalue them. And that is what Mill does," Jackson (1995, 380) argues. "Mill, in short, is cutting off the argument that because women have characteristic X, X is inferior."

If Mary Wollstonecraft argues for a more equal future in which women and men are both more masculine, Mill's view of sex equality deconstructs the artificial divide between (what people take to be) masculine and feminine properties. As young Mill asks in an 1833 letter to Thomas Carlyle, "is there really any distinction between the highest masculine and the highest feminine character?" (1963, 184). Consider a personal example: when John Stuart Mill praised his longtime intellectual partner (and eventual wife) Harriet Taylor, it was not because she was an exemplary woman nor because she was "as good as any man." For Mill, as Nadia Urbinati explains, "She represented the highest level of his human typology because she had 'much feeling and much thought'. She was an example of a human being beyond any gender distinction" (1991, 631). Or as Mill himself put it in his preface to Taylor's 1851 essay "The Enfranchisement of Women," "the foundation of her character was a deep seriousness, resulting from the combination of strongest and most sensitive feelings with the highest principles" (Rossi 1970, 91–92).

Some commentators have attributed Mill's appreciation for the importance of both reason and feeling in part to his philosophical and psychological reaction to the highly rational and intensive education that he received from a young age from his father James Mill and utilitarian luminary Jeremy Bentham (Rossi 1970, 12). It was a lesson in what not to do: as he would later describe it in his *Autobiography* (Mill 1873), this extraordinary education molded young Mill into a cold, logical machine and led to a devastating emotional breakdown. The two things that most spurred his eventual recovery, Mill says, were a new appreciation of the poetry of William Wordsworth and the start of his lifelong relationship with Taylor. After this, "cultivation of the feelings became one of the cardinal points in my ethical and philosophical creed" (Rossi 1970, 18).

When Mill and Taylor met in the early 1830s, he was a bachelor and she a mother of three, five years into a marriage to John Taylor, and they would remain this way for nearly two decades until John Taylor's death in 1849. Harriet and John Stuart Mill wed two years later; seven years after that, Harriet herself died in 1858. But if the marriage was fairly brief, the intellectual partnership was not. In addition to co-authoring several newspaper articles throughout the 1840s and 1850s (Miller 2018), the two worked closely together on *Principles of Political Economy* (1848), "The Enfranchisement of Women" (1851), and *On Liberty* (1859), the last of which Mill would later say "was more directly and literally our joint production than anything else which bears my name" (Mill 1873). Well after Harriet's death, Mill published *The Subjection of Women* (1869), expanding on many of the moral, political, and social-epistemological arguments for sexual equality introduced in "Enfranchisement," which had originally been published without attribution in *The Westminster Review* and was later attributed to "Mrs. John Stuart Mill" when reprinted in 1868 by the Missouri Woman's Suffrage Association (Taylor 1868). Despite the conflicting evidence, Dale Miller notes that "today there seems to be a general consensus that Harriet is the article's primary author" (2018).

Consider this particularly Wollstonecraft-esque passage from "Enfranchisement" on the vicious and virtuous effects that men and women as companions can have on the other's intellectual and moral development:

> Those who are so careful that women should not become men, do not see that men are becoming, what they have decided that women should be—are falling into feebleness which they have so long cultivated in their companions. Those who are associated in their lives, tend to become assimilated in character. In the present closeness of association between the sexes, men cannot retain manliness unless women acquire it. [Rossi 1970, 110]

Both Taylor (1851) and Mill (1869) emphasize that men will change—more specifically, improve—in moving from patriarchal rule to a system of sexual equality. In *The Subjection of Women*, Mill returns to an argument regarding epistemic justification previously made in *On Liberty* (1859, 22). Responsible and reliable belief formation is among an individual's intellectual duties, but not in isolation. Epistemic justification comes from exposing oneself and one's beliefs to real criticism and intellectual engagement by others and fulfilling that same sort of social epistemic function for them in return. Within a patriarchal system, however, boys and men are protected by their gender privilege from having to justify their opinions and ideas, and as a result, develop an inflated sense of their intellectual ability. "Think what it is to be a boy, to grow up to manhood in the belief that without any merit or any exertion of his own…by the mere fact of being born a male he is by right the superior of all and every one of an entire half of the human race," Mill writes. "What must be the effect on his character, of this lesson?" (Rossi 1970, 218). The pervasive unearned gender privilege of men and boys in a patriarchal society is epistemically pernicious. While life will undoubtedly be more challenging for men and boys in an equal society, this challenge is actually a good thing, not only for the women and girls whose opinions will get the fair hearings they deserve but also for their now more epistemically rigorous male counterparts. "The most eminent men cease to improve if they associate only with disciples," Taylor observes. "The mental companionship which is improving, is communion between active minds" (Rossi 1970, 112).

Consider Mill's prediction that, given equality, women would be less self-sacrificing and men more so than they had previously been. It is not that women are naturally more self-abnegating or men are naturally more selfish. A system of gender inequality teaches girls and women that they exist for others—Mill names exaggerated self-abnegation as "the present artificial ideal of feminine character"—while teaching boys and men to see "their own will as such a grand thing that it is actually the law for another rational being" (Rossi 1970, 172). The lesson is not that self-sacrifice is always virtuous or always irrational. Both sexes are misled about their relative importance, and both have room to improve in grounding their actions (self-sacrificing, self-serving, or otherwise) in a more accurate appreciation for women and men as equal beings.

## Human Virtues, Gendered Roles

I do not mean to overstate the differences between Wollstonecraft on one side and Mill and Taylor on the other. As with Wollstonecraft and Macaulay, their similarities are as significant as their differences given how radical their views were compared to contemporary conventional wisdom and how conservative they can seem from a twenty-first-century perspective. Wollstonecraft, Taylor, and Mill are all skeptical of appeals to custom, history, or nature to justify social inequality. All three argue that the social conditions of sexual inequality have vicious effects on the intellectual and moral character of both women and men. Wollstonecraft is perhaps more focused on the ways in which subordination encourages women's tyranny, their use of flattery and guile in the absence of rational discourse between equals. Taylor and Mill focus more on the ways in which unearned superiority gives men an inflated sense of their self-worth and intellectual abilities. But all three writers identify and decry both of these tendencies.

In Taylor and Mill we find echoes of Wollstonecraft's earlier argument that men and women "mutually corrupt and improve" each other. The similarities are perhaps nowhere clearer than in their respective criticisms and defenses of marriage. Wollstonecraft, Taylor, and Mill each discuss ways in which marriage can serve to denigrate or elevate both wives and husbands. With unequal marriage, a family is "a school of despotism, in which the virtues of despotism, but also its vices, are largely nourished" Mill writes. When justly constituted it could instead become a school for sympathy, "the real school of the virtues of freedom" (Rossi 1970, 174–175). Given their visions for ideal marriage as an equal relationship between two people of similar interests and abilities rather than a union of feminine and masculine characters that balance and complement the other, modern readers might wonder whether consistency should have led these early liberal feminist philosophers to support same-sex marriage. But rather than extending marriage to include intimate same-sex relationships, I would suggest that the crux of their position is to extend the virtues of same-sex friendships to include marital relationships. The shared vision is marriage as friendship, where both parties relate to each other as equals, with intimacy and mutual influence, neither with power over the other, nor in control (Solomon & Berggren 1983, 283; Rossi 1970, 233).[1]

Even as Wollstonecraft, Taylor, and Mill envision women and men becoming more similar in temperament and character traits, there are still quite a lot of gendered configurations in social roles and activities throughout their accounts. "Women, I allow, may have different duties to fulfill," Wollstonecraft writes; "but they are *human* duties, and the principles that should regulate the discharge of them, I sturdily maintain, must be the same" (Solomon & Berggren 1983, 301). Masculinity as she envisions and advocates it for women and men is about developing our mental, moral, and physical capacities, but this is not the same thing as women and men *doing* the same things or fulfilling the same sort of functions in a family or society. For their part, Mill and Taylor argue that politics and other spheres of public life should be open to all men and women who show an ability to compete in their chosen sphere. Taylor further argues that it is not only permissible but desirable for women to secure employment outside the home (Rossi 1970, 105). By contrast, Mill says that generally

---

[1] Ruth Abbey (1996, 93, 1999, 80) argues that in modeling marriage on friendship, these authors fail to account for the importance of sexual love in marriage.

speaking it would be best for wives and mothers to refrain from doing so (Rossi 1970, 178–179).

How can Mill's larger commitment to sexual equality square with such an old-fashioned view? On one hand, as Nadia Urbinati puts it, "androgyny forms the philosophical foundation of Mill's vision of civil and political equality between men and women" (1991, 626). The Millian androgyne "was the Individual, the human being's exemplary, the subject of what in *On Liberty* he called *individuality*. It was the sexually blended type that would be developed in discussions with his wife transferred into ethical and political fields" (632). Yet Mill's feminist androgyny seems partial at best in its feminist principles, its underlying notion of androgyny, or both. Urbinati seeks to resolve the apparent contradiction by distinguishing between Mill's principles and his opinions on specific problems. A theme of epistemic humility runs through *The Subjection of Women*. None of us can justifiably claim to know women's and men's true natures, their proper spheres of activity, or that patriarchy is a better social-political system than equality, Mill argues, so long as the artificial conditions of patriarchy have never really been tested against the alternative. Mill allows himself the prediction that "In an otherwise just state of things, it is not, therefore, I think, a desirable outcome, that the wife should contribute by her labour to the income of the family." Immediately after this, he then urges that "the utmost latitude ought to exist for the adaptation of general rules to individual suitabilities; and there ought to be nothing to prevent faculties exceptionally adapted to any other pursuit, from obeying their vocation notwithstanding marriage" (Rossi 1970, 179). Here Mill is acknowledging that his own opinions about what women might do would not be an adequate basis for restrictive social policy. Each person must be free to decide for themselves, not as an inalienable natural right but as the best way to determine the truth of the matter at hand.

## Alternative Masculinities and Feminist Androgynies

In this chapter we explored early feminist responses by liberal political philosophers to a world of sexual division and inequality. The first of these advocated better masculinity for all, in the sense of both social promotion and personal development of rationality, bodily vigor, and independence (which is not to say isolation or antagonism). The second was committed to the value of rationality as well but sought to complement it with emotional development, and more generally, to promote overall human excellence for both women and men through reunification of good human properties that have been artificially divided into masculine and feminine. In highlighting these responses, I do not mean to imply that they are the *only* pathways that are possible as alternatives to patriarchal masculinity. Some might seek a kind of universal normative femininity, for example; others might repudiate manhood or masculinity of all kinds without specifically affirming another option. What is notable about these two responses to patriarchy from early feminist political philosophers is not that they are logically exhaustive, but that between them they presage many of the scholarly and popular alternatives to toxic masculinity that are still advocated today.

In arguing for rational masculinity for women and men, Wollstonecraft sets an early exemplar of a strategy we will see reiterated by a wide variety of writers: the attempt to revise and reclaim an alternative masculinity in contrast to traditional masculinity. The masculinity she advocates for men is (as Abbey puts it) more hypothetical than tautological. Men are not masculine in virtue of being men; in fact, Wollstonecraft was critical of the contemporary condition of most men and so advocated rationality masculinity as better for them. In this her work foreshadows numerous sorts of reclamations of masculinity to come, from conservative to mythopoetic to feminist, which vary considerably but all seek to offer new visions for how we can be better than under the status quo. Wollstonecraft's universal rational masculinity also invites a critical question that will recur in one form or another as we consider these other reclamations of masculinity: namely, why should we conceive of rationality or any other virtuous human quality as part of a revised masculinity, rather than as part of what can help free us from gender altogether?

In Mill's work we find an early, partial sort of feminist androgyny which regards the divisions between masculinity and femininity as artificial and pernicious. Better to remove them and work toward androgyny, toward an ideal of nongendered human well-being that combines the best bits for all of us. This ideal too recurs in both scholarly and popular texts as an appealing escape from patriarchal masculinity. It is this ideal and its appeal, ambiguities, and limitations to which we will turn our attention in the next chapter.

## REFERENCES

Abbey, Ruth. 1996. Odd Bedfellows: Nietzsche and Mill on Marriage. *History of European Ideas* 23 (2–4): 81–104.

———. 1999. Back to the Future: Marriage as Friendship in the Thought of Mary Wollstonecraft. *Hypatia* 14 (3): 78–95.

———. 2019. Masculinity. In *The Wollstonecraftian Mind*, ed. Sandrine Berges, Eileen Hunt Botting, and Alan Coffee, 365–377. New York: Routledge.

Boos, Florence S. 1976. Catherine Macaulay's *Letters on Education*: An Early Feminist Polemic. *The University of Michigan Papers in Women's Studies* 2 (2): 64–78.

Bryson, Valerie. 2003. *Feminist Political Theory*. 2nd ed. New York: Palgrave Macmillan.

Burgess Jackson, Keith. 1995. John Stuart Mill, Radical Feminist. *Social Theory and Practice* 21 (3): 369–396.

Burke, Edmund. (1790) 1890. *Reflections on the Revolution in France*. London: Macmillan.

De Beauvoir, Simone. 1953. *The Second Sex*. Translated by H.M. Pashley. New York: Alfred A. Knopf.

De Bruin-Mole, Megen. 2018. Hail, Mary, the Mother of Science Fiction. *Science Fiction Film and Television* 11 (2): 233–255.

Ford, Thomas H. 2009. Mary Wollstonecraft and the Motherhood of Feminism. *Women's Studies Quarterly* 37 (3–4): 189–205.

Frazer, Elizabeth. 2011. Mary Wollstonecraft and Catharine Macaulay on Education. *Oxford Review of Education* 37 (5): 603–617.

Freedman, Carl. 2002. Hail, Mary: On the Author of 'Frankenstein' and the Origins of Science Fiction. *Science Fiction Studies* 29: 253–264.

Gerson, Gal. 2002. Liberal Feminism: Individuality and Oppositions in Wollstonecraft and Mill. *Political Studies* 50: 794–810.

Gubar, Susan. 1994. Feminist Misogyny: Mary Wollstonecraft and the Paradox of 'It Takes One to Know One'. *Feminist Theory* 20 (3): 453–473.

Johnson, Claudia. 1995. *Equivocal Beings: Politics, Gender, and Sentimentality in the 1790s—Wollstonecraft, Radcliffe, Burney, Austen*. Chicago: University of Chicago Press.

Lewis, Helen. 2020. Mary Wollstonecraft, The Naked Feminist. *The Atlantic*, November 21.

Macaulay, Catharine. (1790) 2014. *Letters on Education*. Cambridge: Cambridge University Press.

Mill, John Stuart. (1833) 1963. The Early Letters of John Stuart *Mill*. In *The Collected Works of John Stuart Mill*, ed. Francis E. Mineka. Toronto: Toronto University Press.

———. (1848) 1965. *Principles of Political Economy*. Reprinted in *The Collected Works of John Stuart Mill*, ed. John M. Robson. Toronto: Toronto University Press.

———. (1859) 1998. *On Liberty and Other Essays*. Oxford: Oxford University Press.

———. (1869) 1984. *The Subjection of Women*. Reprinted in *The Collected Works of John Stuart Mill*, ed. John M. Robson, 259–348. Toronto: Toronto University Press.

———. 1873. *Autobiography*. London: Longmans, Green, Reader, and Dyer.

Miller, Dale E. 2018. Harriet Taylor Mill. *Stanford Encyclopedia of Philosophy*, ed. Edward N. Zalta. https://plato.stanford.edu/archives/spr2019/entries/harriet-mill.

Nussbaum, Martha. 2010. Mill's Feminism: Liberal, Radical, and Queer. In *John Stuart Mill: Thought and Influence*, ed. Paul Kelly and Georgios Varouxakis, 140–155. London: Routledge.

Rossi, Alice, ed. 1970. *Essays on Sex Equality*. Chicago: University of Chicago Press.

Rousseau, Jean Jacques. 1762. *Emile, or On Education*. Translated by Barbara Foxley. Project Gutenberg. https://gutenberg.org/ebooks/5427.

Shelley, Mary. (1818) 2018. *Frankenstein, or A Modern Prometheus*. New York: Penguin Books.

Solomon, Barbara H., and Paula S. Berggren. 1983. *A Mary Wollstonecraft Reader*. New York: New American Library.

Taylor, Harriet. (1851) 1984. The Enfranchisement of Women. Reprinted in *The Collected Works of John Stuart Mill*, ed. John M. Robson, 393–416. Toronto: Toronto University Press.

———. 1868. The Enfranchisement of Women. Reprinted by the Missouri Women's Suffrage Association.

Urbinati, Nadia. 1991. John Stuart Mill on Androgyny and Ideal Marriage. *Political Theory* 19 (4): 626–648.

Wollstonecraft, Mary. 1790. *A Vindication of the Rights of Men*. London: Joseph Johnson.

———. 1792. *A Vindication of the Rights of Woman*. London: Joseph Johnson.

**Open Access**  This chapter is licensed under the terms of the Creative Commons Attribution 4.0 International License (http://creativecommons.org/licenses/by/4.0/), which permits use, sharing, adaptation, distribution and reproduction in any medium or format, as long as you give appropriate credit to the original author(s) and the source, provide a link to the Creative Commons licence and indicate if changes were made.

The images or other third party material in this chapter are included in the chapter's Creative Commons licence, unless indicated otherwise in a credit line to the material. If material is not included in the chapter's Creative Commons licence and your intended use is not permitted by statutory regulation or exceeds the permitted use, you will need to obtain permission directly from the copyright holder.

CHAPTER 3

# Androgyny and the End of Manhood

**Abstract** This chapter considers the appeal and limitations of feminist androgyny and rejections of masculinity as viable alternatives to traditional patriarchal masculinity in the late twentieth century. We explore multiple conceptions of androgyny as more and less compatible with feminist values, revisit John Stoltenberg's repudiation of manhood and masculinity on feminist grounds, and trace how feminist androgyny and refusals of masculinity recur throughout many scholarly and popular accounts of men and manhood. We conclude by considering some notable challenges attendant to Stoltenberg's advice for men of conscience and his account of double vision.

**Keywords** Androgyny • Liberal feminism • Masculinity • Radical feminism • Repudiation of manhood

## Prison Break

"To many feminists, androgyny has come to represent an escape from the prison of gender," writes Mary Anne Warren (1982, 170); "that is, from socially enforced preconceptions of ways in which women and men ought to differ in their psychology and behavior." The ideal of androgyny, "a sex-neutral standard of successful human development," is championed by feminist proponents as a guide for individual men, women, boys, and girls, as well as reassessing and reorganizing social institutions (1982, 173). So conceived, we can see why those who are frustrated with masculinity and committed to feminist values might find androgyny compelling.[1]

As we consider the appeal and limitations of androgyny as a feminist alternative to masculinity, with particular attention to its articulation among feminist philosophers in the late twentieth century, it is worth taking a moment to clarify what was meant (and not meant) by *androgyny*. Some had in mind what Joyce Treblicot (1977) called the *polyandrogynist approach*: that is, when traditionally masculine and traditionally feminine traits and roles are now available to all human beings without limitation or coercion. Each of us would be free to be however we like, gender be damned. While polyandrogyny so construed might promote individual autonomy, critics argued that it was far too sweeping to be a viable feminist ideal. For one thing, it would seem to count both toxic masculinity and the tyrannical femininity that Mary Wollstonecraft described and denounced as consistent with androgyny, so long as a person inhabits the persona in question freely rather than because of social enculturation and enforcement. It would be consistent with people exhibiting all sorts of vicious human character traits as long as such traits are no longer linked to gender. "The polyandrogynist approach is most appropriate with respect to 'feminine' and 'masculine' traits which are largely a matter of personal style and preference," Warren (1982, 178) argued, "and which have little direct moral significance" (see also Timmons and Wasserman 1979).

One might consider instead a sort of *maximalist* ideal of androgyny, where individual humans and social institutions would exhibit all traditionally masculine and traditionally feminine traits. While this would deconstruct the masculine/feminine divide, if taken seriously it would also be unstable and internally incoherent. Masculinity need not be set in strict opposition to femininity, as Shira Tarrant (2009, 88) reminds us, but this does not mean all masculine and feminine traits can coexist either. As a feminist ideal, maximalist androgyny would have the same sorts of issues as polyandrogyny—arguably even worse, since it would not only permit but actively promote truly vicious masculine and feminine traits in individual humans and social institutions.

On the other end of the spectrum would be a uniform idealized androgyny, where all individual humans regardless of biological sex exhibit the same set of traditionally masculine and feminine traits. One might

---

[1] For further feminist advocacy of androgyny, see Bazin and Freeman (1974) and Ferguson (1977); for criticism, see Elshtain (1981) and Morgan (1982).

imagine a parallel sort of uniformity for social systems balancing masculine and feminine traits. This approach could avoid the amoral and anti-feminist implications of the previous two; it would also be meaningfully androgynous in promoting the same set of preferred traits regardless of gender. Unfortunately it would also collapse into the classic dystopian stereotype of an androgynous world without human psychological variation, where everyone thinks and acts exactly the same as everyone else.

For her part Warren was sympathetic to a sort of moral androgyny, wherein ideally masculine and feminine *virtues* are equally distributed and exhibited among human beings regardless of sex. Domestic, political, and other social institutions would be reorganized after this ideal: not to make everyone the same, nor to promote all things masculine and feminine as open to everyone, but to nurture masculine and feminine virtues in everyone. These virtuous character traits are not really masculine and feminine, of course—"not naturally, inevitably, or desirably the monopoly of either sex," Warren (1982, 183–184) writes. "What is artificial is the notion that *combining* these *diverse* capacities is more difficult than *separating* them. This is exactly the myth that the feminist androgynists are attempting to destroy."

James Sterba shares Warren's enthusiasm for feminist androgyny so understood: as he puts it, "other things being equal, the same virtues are appropriate for everyone" (1996, 104). Furthermore, Sterba (1994) argues, explaining feminist justice in terms of the ideal of androgyny can help men to better appreciate its value. It means that feminist justice is not only a negative thing (dismantling male domination or undoing systems of oppression more generally) but also something positive, indeed something constructive. It offers men an ideal to strive for, a better way to be, for ourselves as individuals and for the social institutions that we must reform toward the creation of a gender-free society (1996, 106–107). Such institutions in need of radical restructuring include the family, childcare, education, work schedules, pay inequities, and legal and cultural systems that promote, condone, and ignore violence generally and against women specifically (1994, 177–181).

## I Am (Refusing to Be) a Man

Sterba like Mill grounds his support for androgyny in his liberal feminism, but one need not be a liberal to challenge masculinity on feminist grounds. In *Refusing to be a Man* (1989), *The End of Manhood* (1993), and other writings, John Stoltenberg (2008, 2013) applies the insights and values of radical feminist philosophy to men's lives.[2] His position is clear: manhood is not worth saving. Men and those whom we love would be better off without it: "all we know and recognize as 'manhood'," Stoltenberg insists, "cannot possibly coexist with authentic and passionate and integrated selfhood" (1993, xiv).

Why can't manhood and masculinity be redeemed? For Stoltenberg, it is because being a man essentially requires us "to deny someone else's selfhood–over and over again" (1993, 36). A man concerned with his manhood is concerned with what other men think of him, measuring himself against them and valuing their judgment more than his authentic self. Inhabiting the masculine self can be appealing, given our enduring emotional need for other men's validation, but this manhood "I" is built on seeing and treating women as *less than*. It is both inauthentic and immoral because one cannot consistently make genuine ethical choices and submit to the imperatives of manhood, Stoltenberg argues (1989, 195, 1993, 307). "So long as we continue to try to act in ways that keep us still 'men', we are doomed to paralysis, guilt, self-hatred, inertia," he writes. "So long as we try to act *as men*, in order to continue to *be* men…we doom women to injustice: the injustice that inheres in the very idea that there are two sexes" (1989, 185).

The good news is that we can resist. Manhood is a hoax and refusing to believe in it is an act of resistance to the injustice done in its name. Refusal, Stoltenberg says, "is a personal and political principle of revolutionary liberation beyond any amplitude we can now possibly imagine" (1993, 304). For someone raised to be a man, it is indeed possible to feel better about oneself—not by feeling better about *being a man*, but feeling better about oneself as a conscientiously living *self*. Stoltenberg returns to the challenge of how to live as "men of conscience" throughout his work. Sometimes he is rather pessimistic about this, reflecting on the ways that men of conscience too often focus on making themselves feel better, give into self-conscience paralysis, and otherwise prefer talk to action. At other times he is more optimistic that men of conscience can contribute to bringing about a world of gender justice.

---

[2] As Ken Clatterbaugh puts it, "For radical profeminist men, radical feminism constitutes a set of principles that provide not only the correct analysis of masculinity but also the structures that maintain it" (1997, 51). See Berggren (2014) for an alternate reading of Stoltenberg in post-structuralist feminist terms.

The key claim is that we do not need masculinity in either its traditional patriarchal or revised forms. "Neither cooperation nor domination has to be embedded in gender, however. And really, there is no mandatory requirement for the labels 'masculinity' and 'femininity' in the first place," writes Matthew Gutman (2019, 238). "In the end, we do not need separate traits for masculine and feminine any more than we do for left-handers versus right-handers." Like Stoltenberg, Gutman argues against the search for alternative masculinities—not because traditional masculinity itself is inevitable, but because these gendered concepts are unnecessary, artificial restrictions on how we understand male behavior. Thinking in terms of masculinity and femininity not only provides inadequate explanations of why human beings act as they do, Gutman says, it lets men off the hook and sells men short. Masculinity is an explanatory and agential crutch, without which we can then better understand and evaluate male behavior.

Stoltenberg and Gutman both see masculinity as an impediment to knowing one's true, actually responsible self. On first reading, J.J. Bola seems to defend a similar view in his book *Mask Off: Masculinity Redefined*. "The mask that men have worn for decades, even centuries, has to be fully removed for us to see the true face that lies beneath," Bola writes; "once we remove it, we will see that what lies beneath is a reflection of our true selves, however we choose to be" (2019, 118). But if masculinity is a mask, what exactly does it hide? Is the self that lies beneath it gendered? Bola explains:

> Rather than there being a norm of manhood, people should have the open-mindedness and understanding to realise that there are beautiful variations of manhood and masculinity, and that however a male identity might manifest, that does not make that person more or less of a man. (2019, 73)

Let us unpack this a bit. The metaphor of masculinity as a mask invites two reactions. The first is that masculinity is inauthentic, a façade to be removed, and when it is, then one's true ungendered self previously hidden under the mask is revealed. So when the mask is thrown off, masculinity is thrown off. A second response embraces the mask as performance: our liberation is not necessarily about living mask-free but having the freedom to choose among many masks. Here the problem is not that a mask of masculinity hides the true self; the problem is that one mask has been forced on us. When the mask of hegemonic masculinity is thrown off, men are now free to wear other masks, free to perform other sorts of masculinity.

The vision of unmasking that Bola articulates is, curiously, both and neither of these. He urges us to remove the mask that men have long worn to see our true selves that lie beneath. This means we have true selves, which masks cover up. So when Bola also urges us to embrace the beautiful variations of manhood and masculinity that are possible, these are not new masks we wear instead of the old one. We remove the rigid, limited, one-size-for-all mask of hegemonic masculinity and the true selves beneath are *also* masculine, albeit more diversely so.

## A Gender Reset?

Feminist philosophical scholarship these days is less likely to center around either androgyny or a radical repudiation of manhood and masculinity than in previous decades. A related contemporary phenomenon is the agnostic critical stance on masculinity. What will our future selves look like if—and when—we cast off the shackles of gender generally and patriarchal masculinity specifically? "I don't know," the agnostic says. "Can't see it from here. Whatever it is, it will be better than this." Better in what sense, however, if we cannot even begin to envision the anticipated and advocated alternative to masculinity? In his 2014 book *Love and War*, Tom Digby follows Harriet Taylor and John Stuart Mill in building epistemic humility into his feminist philosophy. "Who knows what gender will look like, or whether it will exist at all," Digby asks, "when men are finally free of sacrificial masculinity and its gendered harm aimed specifically at men?" (2014, 149). Jared Yates Sexton (2019, 252) is likewise confident that patriarchal masculinity is a toxic lie that must be exposed and comparatively less confident about his predictions about what will or should come afterward.

What can be frustrating about this agnostic position is not so much its epistemic humility, the honest ignorance about the future of masculinity, but what we should do and how we should be in what Alison Jaggar (2019) calls *the unjust meantime*. The negative recommendations are clear: cut the cultural puppet strings, stop the cultural programming, and remove the mask of masculinity, the false face that the world tells us we are supposed to present. The agnostic admits that they do not really know what will happen afterward, if and when we individually and collectively have the courage to do this. "But of course saying 'just let go of toxic masculinity' to a man is like saying 'just relax' to a person having a panic attack," Liz Plank observes. "Men will only break free from the masculinity trap when they have a safe alternative" (2019, 118).

Perhaps this is why even someone like Plank who advocates undoing gender at the same time feels compelled to offer a new vision of masculinity. Throughout her book, Plank affirms that she "strongly believe[s] in a world that goes beyond gender" (2019, 33). Against Susan Venker, Plank argues that to "question the ideal that idealized masculinity has instilled is not about telling men to act more like women or women to act more like men; it's about letting everyone be whoever they want" (2019, 111). Later, ruminating on the different things that young men tend to associate with *real men* versus *good men*, Plank writes, "I want to be specific: freeing ourselves from gender rules doesn't mean we have to remove it entirely from our lives, but rather that we take and leave the parts that make sense" (2019, 290).

Each of these emancipatory sentiments is compatible with an aspirational ideal of androgyny. It is curious, then, that Plank concludes her book by making the case for what she calls *mindful masculinity*:

> We need a gender reset, and this is where mindful masculinity comes in as a necessary tool to achieve it…To put it simply, the result is that we become aware of the reason why we do the things we do…Mindful masculinity allows men to ensure that their choices align with the virtues that make them honored to be a man and practice the virtues connected with the things they know to be true. [Plank 2019, 294–295]

We will return to Plank's discussion of mindful masculinity when we consider it as one among several attempted reclamations of masculinity. But for now what is particularly fascinating is the idea that mindful masculinity is a way to free ourselves from gender rules without removing gender from our lives. As Warren (1982, 183) and Sterba (1996, 104) remind us, those virtues traditionally associated with masculinity are still available to men under a feminist ideal of androgyny. Better still, these virtues are not limited to men, and men are not limited to these virtues, worthwhile as they may be. It would seem that mindful masculinity differs from a feminist ideal of androgyny so understood only insofar as, under the former, traditionally feminine virtues are unavailable to men and those virtues that men do practice are framed as masculine rather than as good regardless of gender. If men are indeed mindful and intentional about our choices, not just going through life on gender cruise control (as Plank memorably puts it), then limiting ourselves to those choices that align with masculine virtues seems to be contrary to truly intentional, self-directed living. Mindful androgyny would seem to enable men to do everything Plank wants for us and more.

## Trouble with Double Vision

For his part Stoltenberg is deeply suspicious of the idea of doing something *as men*: "the two most paralyzing words in the vocabulary of the so-called man of conscience" (1989, 182). At the same time, however, he recognizes a kind of pride available to men of conscience, "not in being *men* but in being men *who*…–men who are living their lives in a way that will make a difference" (1989, 198).

I think this distinction can be really helpful, and we'll return to it again in later chapters when we grapple with the paradox of feminist pride in manhood (see Schmitt 2001; Brod 2001). But for Stoltenberg's radical feminist refusal of manhood, this way of characterizing things is pretty confusing. We're not supposed to take pride in being men, to understand ourselves as doing things as men, or for that matter even acquiesce to the "personal and social hoax" (1993, 304) that we *are* men. And yet throughout his work Stoltenberg continues to refer to human beings raised to be men who refuse to believe in manhood as men. What is a man of conscience, if not a man? What are those people who aspire to pride in being men, *who*, if not men? "We need a double vision," Stoltenberg explains. "We need to keep in our mind both the reality of our being men in the sex-class system and the truth of the possibility of a future without it" (1989, 197).

Laid out plainly like this, however, neither half of this conjunction fits easily with Stoltenberg's call to refuse manhood as a matter of justice. There are problems here on psychological, epistemic, conceptual, and political grounds. Take the psychological tension involved in refusing to believe yourself to be a man while also being mindful that you are a man. Is this really possible? Certainly we can refuse to see our manhood as something innate and immutable. With the second half of Stoltenberg's double vision, we can believe in the possibility of a future in which people survive and thrive without being men. But to deny that masculinity is an essential property does not mean it is not a property at all. The first half of Stoltenberg's double vision reminds us that we presently do have this property, even as his call to refuse manhood requires refusing to recognize that.

If the reality is that I am still as yet a man in a gendered world, I would not be a very effective or trustworthy feminist ally for women, non-binary people, or other men if I refuse to acknowledge that reality, just as white people will not be effective or trustworthy allies against white supremacy if they refuse to acknowledge their whiteness and its implications in a racist society. Recall Mill's point about how sexual inequality can foster epistemic arrogance and excessive self-regard among boys and men. If I have been raised and continue to live in that sort of society, I need to be mindful of these moral and intellectual vices as I listen to and collaborate with others. If I am still as yet a man living in an unjust patriarchal society, the gendered configurations of that patriarchal society will continue to confer a diverse array of male privileges upon me. While I do not have to endorse or embrace that, I do need to remember why it is happening. I take it that this is why Stoltenberg advises us to be mindful of our present gendered reality. What is less clear is how this fits with refusing to be a man.

One might argue that refusing to be a man now is a crucial part of making a future world without gender a reality: an instance of being the change you wish to see in the world. I agree that we can't sit idly by and wait for a just world to create itself. As Susan Sherwin reminds us, a commitment to feminism requires not only belief in feminist principles but also active pursuit of changes needed to eliminate oppression (1989). Still it is an open question whether refusing manhood *now* is the right way to bring about a future without manhood. As with any project, the means to bring about a desired end should not be conflated with the end itself, and acting *as if* we have already achieved the end in question is an effective means of achieving such an end only in particular circumstances. Is this one of those circumstances? If we were building the world from scratch, that world could arguably *be genderless* simply by everyone rejecting gender for themselves, how they think about and treat others, and the social institutions they help build and maintain. But ours is a world already steeped in gender oppression, and we cannot hope to achieve a just world without reckoning with historical and extant injustices committed against women, gender non-binary and non-conforming people, and other marginalized and oppressed groups.

Men have individual and collective duties of reparative justice (Walker 2010, 2015) for our part in past and persisting gender injustices, and these cannot be brushed aside in our desire to stop being men. I do not mean to suggest that Stoltenberg is uninterested in reparative justice for historical and contemporary gender injustices; in fact his men of conscience are among those we need to do the work of relational repair. But does refusing to be a man contribute to or detract from reparative work—acknowledging and apologizing for one's responsibility for wrongdoing, making amends toward renewed trustworthiness and possible forgiveness? My worry is that as long as we are men living in a patriarchal society and therefore implicated in, complicit with, and responsible for gender oppression, denying our manhood conflicts with our reparative practices rather than contributing to them. On the other hand, as I seek to demonstrate in the coming chapters, reflecting on and participating in practices of reparative justice for gender oppression can themselves be constitutive of how men embody and perform a distinctly feminist kind of masculinity.

Mary Anne Warren and James Sterba might remind us that feminist androgyny is supposed to be an aspirational *ideal*, a vision of what to work for rather than something to be enacted overnight. This is a fair point; but as with other cases of ideal theorizing in social-political philosophy an ideal is only so useful without some supplemental nonideal direction on how to get there from here (Mills 2005, 168–170). Stoltenberg's advice is to refuse manhood now while remembering that we are still as yet men in a gendered, sexist world. Perhaps this sort of double vision will prove to be the best feminist alternative to toxic masculinity available to us. But given the complications and tensions internal to it, I suggest, the challenge of envisioning and enacting an openly, avowedly feminist masculinity is worth revisiting first.

## References

Bazin, Nancy Toppin, and Alma Freeman. 1974. The Androgynous Vision. *Women's Studies* 2 (2): 185–215.
Berggren, Kalle. 2014. Sticky Masculinity. *Men and Masculinities* 17 (3): 231–252.
Bola, J.J. 2019. *Mask Off: Masculinity Redefined*. London: Pluto Press.
Brod, Harry. 2001. Male Pride and Antisexism. *Men and Masculinities* 3 (4): 405–410.
Clatterbaugh, Ken. 1997. *Contemporary Perspectives on Masculinity*. 2nd ed. Avalon Publishing.
Digby, Tom. 2014. *Love and War: How Militarism Shapes Sexuality and Romance*. New York: Columbia University Press.
Elshtain, Jean Bethke. 1981. Against Androgyny. *Telos* 5 (1): 85–101.

Ferguson, Ann. 1977. Androgyny as an Ideal for Human Development. In *Feminism and Philosophy*, ed. Mary Vetterling-Braggin, Frederick A. Elliston, and Jane English, 45–69. Tottowa, NJ: Rowman & Littlefield.
Gutman, Matthew. 2019. *Are Men Animals? How Modern Masculinity Sells Men Short*. New York: Basic Books.
Jaggar, Alison. 2019. Thinking about Justice in the Unjust Meantime. *Feminist Philosophy Quarterly* 5 (2): 1–24.
Mills, Charles. 2005. 'Ideal Theory' as Ideology. *Hypatia* 20 (3): 165–183.
Morgan, Kathryn Pauly. 1982. Androgyny: A Conceptual Critique. *Social Theory and Practice* 8 (3): 245–283.
Plank, Liz. 2019. *For the Love of Men: A New Vision for Mindful Masculinity*. New York: St. Martin's Press.
Schmitt, Richard. 2001. Proud to Be a Man? *Men and Masculinities* 3 (4): 393–404.
Sexton, Jared Yates. 2019. *The Man They Wanted Me to Be*. Berkeley: Counterpoint.
Sherwin, Susan. 1989. Feminism and Medical Ethics. *Hypatia* 4 (2): 57–72.
Sterba, James. 1994. Feminist Justice and the Pursuit of Peace. *Hypatia* 9 (2): 173–187.
———. 1996. Feminist Justice and Sexual Harassment. *Journal of Social Philosophy* 27 (1): 103–122.
Stoltenberg, John. 1989. *Refusing to be a Man: Essays on Sex and Justice*. London: University College London Press.
———. 1993. *The End of Manhood: A Book for Men of Conscience*. London: Dutton.
———. 2008. Why I Stopped Trying to be a Real Man. *Feminista!* http://www.feminista.com/archives/v1n2/stoltenberg.html.
———. 2013. Why Talking about 'Healthy Masculinity' is Like Talking about 'Healthy Cancer.' *Feminist Current*, August 9.
Tarrant, Shira. 2009. *Men and Feminism*. Berkeley: Seal Press.
Timmons, Mark, and Wayne Wasserman. 1979. Trebilcot on Androgynism. *Journal of Social Philosophy* 10 (2): 1–4.
Treblicot, Joyce. 1977. Two Forms of Androgynism. *Journal of Social Philosophy* 8 (1): 4–8.
Walker, Margaret Urban. 2010. *What is Reparative Justice?* Milwaukee: Marquette University Press.
———. 2015. Making Reparations Possible: Theorizing Reparative Justice. In *Theorizing Transitional Justice*, ed. Claudio Corradetti, Nir Eisikovits, and Jack V. Rotondi, 211–225. London: Ashgate.
Warren, Mary Anne. 1982. Is Androdyny the Answer to Sexual Stereotyping? In *'Masculinity,' 'Femininity,' and 'Androgyny': A Modern Philosophical Discussion*, ed. Mary Vetterling-Braggin, 170–185. Tottowa, NJ: Rowman & Allanheld.

**Open Access** This chapter is licensed under the terms of the Creative Commons Attribution 4.0 International License (http://creativecommons.org/licenses/by/4.0/), which permits use, sharing, adaptation, distribution and reproduction in any medium or format, as long as you give appropriate credit to the original author(s) and the source, provide a link to the Creative Commons licence and indicate if changes were made.

The images or other third party material in this chapter are included in the chapter's Creative Commons licence, unless indicated otherwise in a credit line to the material. If material is not included in the chapter's Creative Commons licence and your intended use is not permitted by statutory regulation or exceeds the permitted use, you will need to obtain permission directly from the copyright holder.

CHAPTER 4

# Feminist Reclamations of Masculinity

**Abstract** Resistance to discarding manhood and masculinity comes from not only conservatives but also avowed feminists like bell hooks, who sought to reclaim masculinity as not just compatible with but grounded in feminist values and projects. We turn in this chapter to feminist reclamations of masculinity, most notably (though not limited to) hooks' *We Real Cool* and *The Will to Change*. There is a lot to admire in these efforts to reclaim feminist masculinity; much of what they identify as constituting better, more just, more mindful masculinity are indeed good human qualities. Yet as a viable guide for feminist men, these accounts fall short in one way or another.

**Keywords** bell hooks • Feminist masculinity • Justice • Partnership • Patriarchy • Visionary feminism

Not all resistance to rejecting masculinity and embracing androgyny has come from those who are antagonistic to feminism. bell hooks is one visionary feminist who has warned against discarding manhood or masculinity too quickly. In *Feminism is for Everyone* (2000), *We Real Cool* (2004a), and *The Will to Change* (2004b), she sees feminist masculinity as a loving alternative to patriarchal masculinity. "Undoubtedly," hooks says, "one of the first revolutionary acts of visionary feminism must be to restore maleness and masculinity as an ethical biological category" (2004b, 114).

There is much to admire in hooks' and others' efforts to reclaim masculinity; many of the things they identify as constitutive of a better kind of masculinity are indeed virtuous human qualities. In the later chapters of this book, I try to follow their lead in locating feminist masculinity between hegemonic patriarchal masculinity on one side and feminist rejections of masculinity on the other. But as written, these accounts of feminist masculinity are crucially incomplete; key theoretical and practical questions remain unanswered. Can feminist masculinity offer us a meaningful alternative to feminist androgyny while recognizing and respecting the diversity of men's, women's, and non-binary people's experiences and identities? What makes love, justice, empathy, courage, or other virtuous qualities constitutive of feminist masculinity without presuming that masculinity is just whatever male people happen to do? Addressing these questions will find us both building on and going beyond these existing visions of feminist masculinity.

## Envisioning Feminist Masculinity

bell hooks long championed a vision of feminist change in which men can play productive roles as comrades in struggle (1984, 67). Her vision is grounded in two claims that are sometimes seen as conflicting: that patriarchy oppresses women *and* harms women and men. "These two realities co-exist" (1984, 73).[1] In emphasizing these simple but vital ideas and their interconnections, hooks takes herself to diverge from defenders of traditional masculinity and many feminist critics, both of whom assume that because patriarchy and feminism are inherently incompatible, this means that feminism has nothing to offer men and men have nothing to offer feminism. But this is to conflate patriarchy and masculinity. "The crisis facing men is not the crisis of masculinity," hooks explains, "it is a crisis of patriarchal masculinity. Until we make this distinction clear, men will continue to fear that any critique of patriarchy represents a threat" (2004b, 32).

Her defense of feminist masculinity did not mean hooks was unsympathetic to the presumptive conflict between men's happiness and women's

---

[1] As Alison Bailey (2021, 6) reminds us, "All persons who are oppressed are harmed, but not all persons who are harmed are oppressed."

liberation. "I often wished the men in my life would die," she writes. "Women and children all over the world want men to die so that they can live. This is the most painful truth of male domination" (2004b, xv). Yet male-exclusionary feminism fails to acknowledge another important truth—"that we need men in our lives, that men are in our lives, whether we want them to be or not, that we need men to challenge patriarchy, that we need men to change" (2004b, xvi). This continues a theme from *Feminism is for Everyone*: "activists who call on all women to reject men refused to look at either the caring bonds women shared with men or the economic and emotional ties (however positive or negative) that bind women to men who are sexist" (2000, 69). Indeed, even in her earliest work hooks criticized male-exclusionary feminism not only for failing to envision loving alternatives to patriarchy but also for reflecting the unacknowledged race-based and class-based privileges of bourgeois white women. She takes up a more intersectional view of race, class, and gender grounded in recognition of black women's and men's shared experiences of collective action:

> There is a special tie binding people together who struggle collectively for liberation. Black women and men have been united by such ties. It is the experience of shared resistance struggle that led black women to reject the anti-male stance of some feminist activists. (1984, 69)

hooks returns throughout her work to stories of men in her life who have been not just disappointed but devalued and degraded by a dominator model of manhood; "the primary genocidal threat, the force that endangers black male life," she writes, "is patriarchal masculinity" (2004a, 32).

bell hooks described herself as a visionary feminist for a reason. For her, the beliefs that men have nothing to offer feminism and feminism has nothing to offer men both stem from the absence of a clear vision of what feminist manhood might look like. Patriarchy is invested in obscuring any such vision, hooks argues, and for far too long feminism has failed to adequately articulate one. "How can you become what you cannot imagine?" she asks (2000, 32). This emphasis on the need for alternative forms of masculinity is rooted not only in solidarity with other women but also her love for men with whom she stands in relationships of interdependency, men like her grandfather, her brother, her longtime partner, and her students. In *The Will to Change*, hooks shares a story of a student struggling with how to follow the example set by his father:

> He tells me and the other men who sit in our circle of love, 'I just think of what my father would do and do the opposite.' Everyone laughs. I affirm this practice, adding only that it is not enough to stay in the space of reaction, that being simply reactive is always to risk allowing that shadowy past to overtake the present. (2004b, 10)

hooks contends that men can and do benefit by challenging presumptive gender roles. Yet the sort of challenge that she envisions cannot merely reshuffle and react to traditional masculinity: it must face and critique patriarchy directly. This was her issue with the mythopoetic men's movement of the 1990s, which "did not consistently demand that men challenge patriarchy or envision liberating models of masculinity" (2004b, 113). If these reclamations of masculinity fall short, so too do pro-feminist calls to give up masculinity entirely. To those who "suggest that we need to do away with the term, that we need 'an end to manhood'," hooks objects that "such a stance furthers the notion that there is something inherently evil, bad, or unworthy about maleness" (2004b, 115). This notion is contrary to feminist love for men and boys and so contrary to her vision for feminist masculinity.

We can see hooks' positive vision of masculinity in her contrast between models of domination and models of partnership (see also Collins 2006, 91–93):

> To offer men a different way of being, we must first replace the dominator model with a partnership model that sees interbeing and interdependency as the organic relationship of all living beings. In the partnership model selfhood, whether one is female or male, is always at the core of one's identity. Patriarchal masculinity teaches males to be pathologically narcissistic, infantile, and psychologically dependent for self-definition on the privileges (however relative) that they receive from having been born male... In a partnership model male identity like its female counterpart would be centered around the notion of an essential goodness that is inherently relationally oriented. (2004b, 117)

hooks further articulates her vision of feminist masculinity as nondominating, loving masculinity with particular emphasis on the value of interdependency:

> Feminist masculinity presupposes that it is enough for males to be to have value, that they do not have to 'do,' to 'perform,' to be affirmed and loved. Rather than defining strength as 'power over,' feminist masculinity defines strength as one's capacity to be responsible for self and others. This strength is a trait males and females need to possess. (2004b, 117)

Building upon Olga Silverstein's characterization of feminist masculinity as chiefly constituted by integrity, self-love, emotional awareness, assertiveness, relational skill, and capacities for empathy, autonomy, and interconnection, hooks identifies "the core of feminist masculinity" as a "commitment to gender equality and mutuality as crucial for interbeing and partnership in the creating and sustaining of life" (2004b, 118).

What emerges in these passages is an alternative to masculinity as domination, one that resists the move to androgyny and does so on explicitly feminist grounds. Where patriarchy demands that "real men must prove their manhood by idealizing aloneness and disconnection," masculinity as hooks envisions it enables men to see themselves differently, "that they become more real through the act of connecting with others, through building community" (2004b, 121). So understood, men enact and embody feminist masculinity through active and loving participation in relationships of reciprocity, mutuality, and interdependence.

## Real Men and Just Guys

If bell hooks came to the reclamation of masculinity through her commitment to loving, visionary feminism, other scholars have arrived at a similar destination through their work in masculinities and men's studies. Michael Kimmel is one such particularly influential figure, having contributed to the sociology of men and masculinity in scholarly and popular books, edited collections, public lectures, and his work with the National Organization of Men against Sexism (NOMAS). Kimmel has consistently identified himself and his work as profeminist and reaffirmed the importance of centering gender studies on the feminist recognition of women's systematic oppression and men's systematic privilege.[2] The idea that men as beneficiaries of sexism are fundamentally incompatible with feminism is a serious problem, Kimmel says. "To be a man means to be an oppressor. Thus we—men who could support feminism—cannot be said to exist if the polar dichotomy by which they see the world is to remain in place" (1998, 61). The concern is not that men are inescapably anti-feminist but that because gender privilege is "indelibly inscribed onto men, and men embody it whether they choose to or not, then the only possibility for men to be redeemed is for them to renounce masculinity itself. One simply cannot be a man and support feminism" (1998, 63.)

Here Kimmel is voicing (though not himself endorsing) a position incompatible with feminist masculinity, one allowing only for men's repudiation of masculinity or strict political delineation between men and women. Kimmel himself is more optimistic that men can constructively take up the problem of male privilege:

> Pro-feminism, a position that acknowledges men's experience without privileging it, possesses the tools to both adequately analyze men's aggregate power, and also describe the ways in which individual men are both privileged by that social level of power and feel powerless in the face of it. (1998, 64)

Throughout his work Kimmel characterizes masculinity as ever changing and manhood as socially constructed while challenging the assumption that manhood and masculinity must be inimical to feminist values. Rebuking "the implicit equation of manhood with oppression and inequality–as if real men support injustice" (1998, 67), Kimmel's positive view of masculinity is that *really real* men support justice.

---

[2] In August 2018, reports of sexual harassment and professional misconduct were made against Kimmel by multiple former graduate students, detailing unwelcome sexual advances, deadnaming trans scholars, and inequitable treatment of straight male vs. female, queer, and non-binary students (Flaherty 2018). Kimmel's response at the time was that he took the charges seriously and would "make amends to those who believe I have injured them" (Mangan 2018), but since then he has made no public apology nor acknowledgment of wrongdoing. Whether scholars should avoid citing or engaging with his work in light of these reports and his subsequent silence is a difficult question (Flood 2018; Jensen 2018; McCourt 2019), but at present I am unaware of any general call to do so. My own discussion of Kimmel on manhood and masculinity is intended to be critical and dialectical rather than an appeal to his intellectual or moral authority.

This identification of real, good manhood with ethics and justice carries through into *Guyland*, Kimmel's popular critical appraisal of American manhood today for mostly straight, white, middle and upper-class men in the years before, during, and after their time spent at four-year universities. "Guyland" as Kimmel theorizes it is a relatively recent socio-historical phenomenon, an arrested development between adolescence and adulthood and (not unrelatedly) a notably gendered period of life. Masculinity in Guyland is constantly policed by other men and tightly prescribed as both not-feminine and not-gay. Women are indirectly yet significantly affected as well, Kimmel argues, insofar as their own sexualities and relationships with the guys of Guyland are tightly prescribed and limited accordingly.

The central question for Kimmel is not how to avoid Guyland, which is a stage of development, but rather how to make the constructive transition from Guyland into adulthood in better ways. Here adulthood is understood in traditional demographic terms: completing education, holding a job, getting married, having kids, moving out of one's parents' house, and so on (2008, 122). In envisioning men's healthy transitions out of Guyland masculinity, Kimmel contrasts "just" guys with just guys: "guys who are capable of acting ethically, of doing the right thing, of standing up to the centripetal pull of Guyland. Guys can become everyday heroes. They can actually become men" (2008, 267).

Manhood so conceived becomes associated with achieving adulthood and doing the right thing. The "new model" of masculinity with which Kimmel concludes *Guyland* is put in these terms:

> [B]eing a real man is not going along with what you know in your heart to be cruel, inhumane, stupid, humiliating, and dangerous. Being a real man means doing the right thing, standing up to immorality and injustice when you see it, and expressing compassion, not contempt, for those who are less fortunate. In other words, it's about being courageous. (2008, 287)

Notice how this new model of masculinity retains a normative aspiration, where virtues of courage and compassion are gendered for "real men." Kimmel echoes and expands the "new definition of masculinity for a new century" that he previously sketched in *Manhood in America*. In the earlier text, Kimmel argued for democratic manhood distinct from traditional masculinity *and* androgyny, the latter of which he characterized as "blurring of masculinity and femininity into a mélange of some vaguely defined human qualities" (1996, 334). Democratic manhood is instead composed of old and new "masculine virtues" including compassion, nurturing, egalitarianism, dependability, self-reliance, strength, purpose, and a commitment to justice and ethical action.

Where mythopoetic men like Robert Bly (1990) and Sam Keen (1992) insist that initiation into wild-manhood can only be led by other men, Kimmel is happy to acknowledge the important roles that women play in guiding guys into manhood/adulthood (2008, 272). But he also emphasizes that fathers have a special duty to resist their own temptations of regression. "When fathers resist the urge to identify with Guyland," Kimmel says, "they can model empathic manhood and enrich their sons' lives with a concrete example of what honor and integrity look like [and] show their sons that there are real alternatives to Guyland in which responsibility and accountability and self-respect are qualities that should be strived for" (2008, 277).

## MAKING MASCULINITY MEANINGFUL

hooks and Kimmel exhibit perceptive attention to men's relationships to feminism; both identify and seek to defend sensible, valuable qualities for men as constructive alternatives to patriarchal masculinity. As we think about how to differentiate feminist masculinity from not only traditional forms of masculinity but also androgyny and femininity, however, a curious problem remains. Let us agree that courage, compassion, empathy, self-love, opposition to injustice, and a commitment to gender equality are valuable human qualities, and certainly important for the pursuit of feminist change. Let us also agree that many men lack such qualities, in part because patriarchal masculinity frames them as incompatible with real manhood. What remains as yet unclear is how these feminist alternatives are meaningfully constitutive of *masculinity*. Why should we see men who embody and enact such qualities as performing a kind of masculinity rather than embodying and enacting gender non-specific human virtues?

The answer is not that only male people can or even should embody these qualities, of course. For her part, hooks explicitly sees the partnership model as something both women and men can and should participate in, such that "male identity, like its female counterpart, would be centered around the notion of an essential goodness that is inherently relationally oriented." In arguing that feminist masculinity defines strength as "one's capacity to be responsible for self and others," she also sees strength-as-responsibility as "a trait males and females need to possess" (hooks 2004b, 117). Feminist masculinity for hooks is built around a deep commitment to gender equality and mutuality, and yet she also recognizes this commitment as important for feminist women too. How then do men become "more real" by participating in community-building and interconnection, on this view of feminist manhood, if this work and interconnection are also constitutive of feminist womanhood? To the extent that these worthy qualities and practices are identified and advanced as worthwhile for women *and* men, how do they give meaning to a kind of feminist masculinity rather than, say, a feminist ideal of androgyny?

Recall Sterba's description of feminist androgyny as "a broader base ideal for both women and men that combines virtues and desirable traits traditionally associated with women with virtues and desirable traits traditionally associated with men" (1998, 292). The feminist reclamation of masculinity that hooks advocates would seem to do this: it rejects traditionally masculine traits of domination and disconnection and embraces traits of empathy, mutuality, and self-love. hooks recognizes these traits as necessary for female as well as male people, which makes her caution against calls for an end to manhood and her characterization of the embodiment of such traits as a kind of masculinity puzzling. Here I echo River Fagan's simultaneous appreciation for hooks and critical assessment that her account of masculinity "seemed to be simply a description of a healthy person not a healthy man; nothing in it felt specific to manhood or masculinity" (2013, 37).

The puzzle is no easier when we turn to Kimmel's vision of just guys, democratic manhood, and a model of masculinity in which acting ethically, doing the right thing, and standing up to injustice are ways that guys become better men. For example, being a "real man" is about courage, and yet Kimmel surely will agree that women can be courageous and stand up for justice too, and it is not as though in being courageous these women thereby embody or perform masculinity. Such virtues are not distinctive of masculinity and manhood as Kimmel recommends them, even as they are presented as constitutive of masculinity and manhood as he articulates them.

A recent exchange between Kimmel and Lisa Wade on toxic masculinity shows how slippery things can get. Here Kimmel notes that admirable traits such as honor, integrity, accountability, and doing the right thing are frequently associated with men and masculinity. He is happy to make use of those associations in conversations about "what it means to be a good man," and yet he also recognizes that these really are just good human traits (Kimmel and Wade 2018, 238). "I think what we want to do is gradually, over time, we need to degender those ideas because being a good man is being a good person" (2018, 249). While reasonable, "it also sounds like a way of tricking men," Wade cautions. "So have we given them a good place to land *as men?*" (2018, 249, emphasis original). Here it seems to me that Wade is asking Kimmel whether there is anything to his recommendations for good, just manhood and masculinity beyond their rhetorical functions, and Kimmel for his part declines to reassure her otherwise:

> I think when we were talking about being a good man, that those really were traits that we would agree–you and I would agree–were about being a good person. I think men still experience that in a very gendered way. They think that's about manhood, and I'm okay with them thinking that and expanding the definition. [2018, 251]

If his discussions of what it means to be a good man are mainly rhetorical rather than substantive, some might see in Kimmel's account of what it takes to escape Guyland and achieve adulthood in terms of traditional markers of success (degree, job, wife, kids, home) something more distinctive of manhood specifically. Recall his characterization of fathers modeling their manhood in terms of taking responsibility. But taking that route would seem to lead back to some sort of traditional patriarchal masculinity rather than to a meaningfully feminist alternative. Associating manhood with adulthood as typically conceived is problematic for at least two reasons. It both disassociates these markers of success from women or gender non-binary people who might value and achieve them and undermines the manhood of those men blocked by homophobia, classism, racism, and other forms of oppression from attaining success so defined.

An ideal of androgyny capable of grounding a visionary feminism in which all women and men are free to organize their lives and relationships entirely unconstrained by gender seems especially fitting for bell hooks' emancipatory aspirations. She returns throughout her work to the need to grant boys "the same rights as girls" and for boys and men "every right that we desire for girls and women" (2000, 71, 2004b, 111). She locates the start of her own critical thinking on maleness in childhood, specifically in witnessing the distinctly gendered ways in which she and her brother were treated. "Although we were often confused, we knew one fact for certain: we could not be and act the way we wanted to, doing what we felt like. It was clear to us that our behavior had to follow a predetermined, gendered script" (2004b, 19). hooks describes how this development was bad not only for her but her brother too, forced as he was to harden himself and close himself off from emotion. What comes through clearly in her account is a longing for that time before gender was introduced to and prescribed for them, a time when sister and brother were both free to follow their childhood muses.

Yet hooks also emphatically insists that there is something worth saving in maleness, manhood, and masculinity divorced from patriarchy. The "essential goodness of male being" (2004b, 33), "essential goodness of maleness" (124), and "affirmation of that which is positive and potentially positive in male being" (166) play a significant role in her thinking. It is something that male-exclusionary feminism ignores, patriarchy masculinity cannot admit, and visionary feminism must celebrate. "Male being, maleness, masculinity must stand for the essential core goodness of the self, of the human body that has a penis," hooks maintains. Contrary to feminist repudiations of masculinity, she champions "a creative loving response that can separate maleness and manhood from all the identifying traits patriarchy has imposed on the self that has a penis" (114–115). But where exactly does this leave us?

One might try to frame the various admirable qualities that hooks and Kimmel each identify as constituting an alternative masculinity rather than patriarchal masculinity or genderless humanity by stipulating that such qualities are constitutive of masculinity just in case they are embodied by men or boys. To express the idea somewhat formally, a trait or quality $x$ is taken to be constitutive of masculinity, even though it is not unique to those who are masculine, because $x$ is stipulated as constitutive of masculinity when it is associated with a male human body. For example, we could identify courage, love, and empathy as part of feminist masculinity while recognizing that women and gender non-binary people are also courageous, loving, and empathic without this making them masculine as a result because being courageous, loving, or empathic is (so the argument goes) only masculinizing for men and boys.

I worry that this sort of reclaimed masculinity has significant problems on both conceptual and feminist grounds, however. Beyond bald stipulation, it does not seem to meaningfully differentiate between masculinity so defined and an ideal of androgyny. Both allow that everyone can be wise, courageous, caring, and so on; then this model of feminist masculinity rather superfluously insists that these things are masculine for men and boys. In that case, what has the repudiation of manhood and masculinity lost that this conception of feminist masculinity retains? bell hooks is committed to disentangling maleness and manhood from patriarchal masculinity for many reasons, among which is the need for feminist love—to love men and boys, and to enable men and boys to love. And yet to affirm that men and boys *as human persons* deserve love and are capable of love does not require *loving maleness*. To affirm that men and boys like women and girls have within us an "essential core goodness of the self" does not require an "essential goodness of male being," unless we can explain how maleness is essential to the core self of those socialized to be men and boys. This of course is exactly what feminist analyses of manhood mean to challenge.

We may further worry that this attempt to reframe masculinity is at odds with the identities and lived experiences of many men, women, and gender non-binary people. hooks' repeated evocation of "the human body that has a penis" as synonymous with maleness and manhood would seem to presume that one's gender identity can simply be read off one's anatomy. Yet not all men self-identify as biologically male, nor do all men have a penis, nor do all those who have a penis identify as men. On its own having a penis is neither necessary nor sufficient for being a man, which makes this a shaky foundation upon which to build an alternative to toxic masculinity. Whatever a viable feminist reclamation of masculinity is going to look like, it cannot deny masculinity of trans men who choose not to (or have yet to) pursue anatomical change, nor presumptively foist manhood or masculinity onto all human persons with so-called male anatomy. Such implications would fall short of even the most minimal requirements for intersex- and trans-positive feminist theorizing (e.g., Fausto-Sterling 2000; Heyes 2003; Bettcher 2014). If we are going to follow hooks in reclaiming masculinity on feminist grounds, we will need to be able to account for what makes it both meaningfully, distinctively feminist and meaningfully, distinctively masculine.

## Mindful (of) Masculinity

This challenge for hooks and Kimmel also holds for other recent reclamations of masculinity that are, if not explicitly feminist themselves, then at least critical of traditional masculinity and neutral or sympathetic to feminism. Recall Liz Plank's advocacy of mindful masculinity in her 2019 book

*For the Love of Men*. Plank makes it clear that she believes in a world beyond gender, but at the same time she sees a need for positive masculinity. In the conclusion of her book, Plank draws this lesson from a conversation with Michael Kimmel, that "masculinity wasn't toxic, it was the monster masquerading as masculinity that was" (2019, 289). She continues:

> It's by attending to masculinity that we can heal it. Mindful masculinity is how we can cleanse it from all the lies it's been associated with. It encourages men to look inward to remain connected to all those things that make them a good man instead of the unhelpful trash they've inadvertently absorbed and are carrying around about what it means to be a 'real man.' Being mindful about our gender means we awaken ourselves to the habits and behaviors we've automatically come to identify with and choose which ones serve us and which ones don't. [294]

Plank is urging men to be mindful, intentional rather than passive about our habits and behaviors, and with this I couldn't agree more. But if mindful masculinity is not about shunning masculinity but rather claiming it back, what is being reclaimed? Courage, self-awareness, and control of one's emotions and one's mental health are identified with mindful masculinity, yet Plank would surely agree that these qualities are equally available to women and non-binary people. The question that goes unanswered is why we should see these human qualities as masculine-making and why men's mindfulness is best understood as a reset of gender rather than a way to move beyond it.

Edward Adams and Ed Frauenheim attempt a similar reclamation project in their 2020 book *Reinventing Masculinity*, which begins with a critical analysis of the "confined masculinity" that characterizes men's lives today and throughout much of human history. Confined masculinity is overly rigid and traditional, outdated and unhealthy. "It is a constrained conception of masculinity, one in which men tend to define themselves as playing just a few dominant roles—the protector, the provider, and the conqueror" (Adams and Frauenheim 2020, Introduction). These roles do have a place, they argue, as do traditional masculine traits like strength, valor, and courage, when they are incorporated into a more expansive, interconnected, liberating conception of masculinity. This "liberating masculinity" as they envision it is quite comfortable with men being tender and caring, comfortable with women being assertive and autonomous, and also comfortable with (though not limited to) the aforementioned roles of confined masculinity. Most of all, Adams and Frauenheim explain, it is a shift from "me" thinking to "me and we" thinking:

> Instead of the self-absorption found in confined masculinity, a liberating man recognizes the impact of his actions or inactions on others. He therefore applies his courage, might, and perseverance in service to others. In this way, liberating masculinity is a virtuous masculinity. (2020, Introduction)

To traditional masculine behaviors like confidence, competition, and physical courage, liberating masculinity will add curiosity, compassion, and commitment to personal growth. At times Adams and Frauenheim sound like hooks: "Liberating masculinity is virtuous and relational. It is virtuous because it espouses positive actions that are of benefit to both the self and others; and it's relational because it recognizes that everything is interconnected" (2020, Ch. 2). This sort of reinvention of masculinity is nontoxic, good for ourselves, and good for those with whom we are interconnected and interdependent.

The challenge facing liberating masculinity is similar to one we raised for Kimmel's democratic manhood. Adams and Frauenheim are not just *describing* a change they see among modern men but *advocating* liberating masculinity as a better way for men to be men. Consider for example the place for traditionally patriarchal roles of the protector and provider in this reimagined masculinity. If these now-transformed roles as the authors envision them are open not only to men but people generally, then either those who perform these roles thereby participate in liberating masculinity or they do not. Like Wollstonecraft on rational masculinity, Adams and Frauenheim could extend liberating masculinity to men, women, and non-binary people who act as protectors and providers. This does not seem to be their intent, however, so it then seems arbitrary to identify these social roles as part of a liberating masculinity when men perform them but not when other people do so. Adams and Frauenheim could restrict their reimagined versions of protector and provider roles to men only, but then this not-so-new spin on traditional masculinity would contradict their crucial claim that liberating masculinity is also supportive of women's autonomy, of their freedom to live their lives as they themselves choose.

It is worth noting that confining and liberating masculinity are modeled after Shoma Morita's concepts of the confined and extended selves. Adams and Frauenheim happily acknowledge the debt. But as the extended self that Morita describes does not seem to be meaningfully gendered, this then raises the question why confined men should not work toward a gender-free liberating extended self rather than reimagined masculinity. The conceptual confusion extends to individual character traits. Consider compassion, for example, which Adams and Frauenheim describe both as a "gender-free trait" (2020, Conclusion) and "at the heart of essential masculine traits" (2020, Ch. 2) for liberating masculinity. Can it be both? Like air and water, compassion is indeed vital for men and for all people regardless of gender. It can be useful, even liberating to identify compassion as something that differentiates traditional masculinity from the nontoxic alternative(s) we seek. What remains mysterious, however, is how it could be at once essentially masculine and also gender-free.

"Being a real man doesn't have to mean setting oneself up in binary opposition to femininity," writes Shira Tarrant (2009, 88). "Real masculinity can involve valuing a wide range of emotions, experiences, preferences, desires, and accomplishments of all people." If masculinity is worth saving, Tarrant is surely right about this, and I fully agree that masculinity need not be set in binary opposition to femininity. Depending on how we make sense of these ideas, one person can embody, perform, or otherwise participate in masculinity, femininity, neither or both of them. The recurring challenge for multiple recent reclamations of masculinity is when a property or activity is taken to be constitutive of masculinity as opposed to abandoning masculinity even as that *same* property or activity is acknowledged as equally compatible with non-masculinity in others. This challenge of differentiation may not be an insurmountable problem, but it is one that a consistent, meaningful account of feminist masculinity must reckon with.

## References

Adams, Edward, and Ed Frauenheim. 2020. *Reinventing Masculinity: The Liberating Power of Compassion and Connection.* Oakland: Berrett-Koehler.
Bailey, Alison. 2021. *The Weight of Whiteness.* Lanham: Lexington Books.
Bettcher, Talia. 2014. Feminist Perspectives on Trans Issues. In *Stanford Encyclopedia of Philosophy, ed.* Edward: N. Zalta. https://plato.stanford.edu/entries/feminism-trans/.
Bly, Robert. 1990. *Iron John: A Book about Men.* Boston: Addison-Wesley.

Collins, Patricia Hill. 2006. In *A Telling Difference: Dominance, Strength, and Black Masculinities. In Progressive Black Masculinities*, ed. D. Mutua Athena, 73–97. New York: Routledge.

Fagan, River Willow. 2013. The Bullying Demands of Masculinity. In *Men Speak Out*, ed. Shira Tarrant. New York: Routledge.

Fausto-Sterling, Anne. 2000. *Sexing the Body: Gender Politics and the Construction of Sexuality*. New York: Basic Books.

Flaherty, Colleen. 2018. More than Rumors. *Inside Higher Ed*, August 10.

Flood, Michael. 2018. When Profeminist Men are Alleged to Have Perpetrated Abuse or Harassment. *XY*, August 7.

Heyes, Cressida. 2003. Feminist Solidarity after Queer Theory. *Signs* 28 (4): 1093–1120.

hooks, bell. 1984. *Feminist Theory: From Margin to Center*. Boston: South End.

———. 2000. *Feminism Is for Everybody: Passionate Politics*. London: Pluto Press.

———. 2004a. *We Real Cool: Black Men and Masculinity*. New York: Atria Books.

———. 2004b. *The Will to Change: Men, Masculinity, and Love*. New York: Atria Books.

Jensen, Robert. 2018. What are the Responsibilities of Profeminist Men in the Michael Kimmel Case? *Feminist Current*, August 6.

Keen, Sam. 1992. *Fire in the Belly: On Being a Man*. New York: Bantam Books.

Kimmel, Michael. 1996. *Manhood in America*. New York: The Free Press.

———. 1998. Who's Afraid of Men Doing Feminism? In *Men Doing Feminism*, ed. Tom Digby. New York: Routledge.

———. 2008. *Guyland*. New York: HarperCollins.

Kimmel, Michael, and Lisa Wade. 2018. Ask a Feminist: Michael Kimmel and Lisa Wade Discuss Toxic Masculinity. *Signs* 44 (1): 233–254.

Mangan, Katherine. 2018. 'I Want to Hear Those Charges': Noted Sociologist Defers Award Until He Can 'Make Amends'. *Chronicle of Higher Education*, August 1.

McCourt, Molly. 2019. Academic Activism. *Thinking C21*, March 4. https://www.c21uwm.com/2019/03/04/academic-activism-grappling-with-the-scholarship-of-sexual-harassers-in-the-metoo-era/.

Plank, Liz. 2019. *For the Love of Men: A New Vision for Mindful Masculinity*. New York: St. Martin's Press.

Sterba, James. 1998. Is Feminism Good for Men and Are Men Good for Feminism? In *Men Doing Feminism*, ed. Tom Digby. New York: Routledge).

Tarrant, Shira. 2009. *Men and Feminism*. Berkeley: Seal Press.

**Open Access**  This chapter is licensed under the terms of the Creative Commons Attribution 4.0 International License (http://creativecommons.org/licenses/by/4.0/), which permits use, sharing, adaptation, distribution and reproduction in any medium or format, as long as you give appropriate credit to the original author(s) and the source, provide a link to the Creative Commons licence and indicate if changes were made.

The images or other third party material in this chapter are included in the chapter's Creative Commons licence, unless indicated otherwise in a credit line to the material. If material is not included in the chapter's Creative Commons licence and your intended use is not permitted by statutory regulation or exceeds the permitted use, you will need to obtain permission directly from the copyright holder.

CHAPTER 5

# Allyship and Feminist Masculinity

**Abstract** Despite the issues raised about feminist reclamations of masculinity in the prior chapter, I believe bell hooks was right to emphasize the relevance of relationality, intentionality, and justice to an alternate vision of manhood. We can indeed make sense of normative feminist masculinity, such that men as men have distinctive, constructive contributions to make to feminist work. Much like feminist androgyny, feminist allyship masculinity seeks to upend masculinity as a received social category, while also diverging with feminist androgyny in emphasizing men's specific yet non-essentialist contributions to feminist projects.

**Keywords** Allyship • Feminist philosophy • Identity • Masculinity • Social location • Whiteness

## THE WHITENESS PROBLEM

Let us begin by looking to Linda Alcoff's work on white anti-racism as a fruitful comparison for making sense of the possibility of normative feminist masculinity. In particular, let us consider how Alcoff addresses what she calls *the question of white identity*:

> But what is it to acknowledge one's whiteness? Is it to acknowledge that one is inherently tied to structures of domination and oppression, that one is

irrevocably on the wrong side? In other words, can the acknowledgement of whiteness produce only self-criticisms, even shame and self-loathing? Is it possible to feel okay about being white? (2006, 206)

Avowed white supremacists might feel okay about being white, but what about white people who are committed to anti-racism? Alcoff holds that each of us needs some felt connection with a larger community, some history beyond ourselves to avoid falling into nihilism and stay invested in the value of social progress. While it is understandable that anti-racist whites might wish to disavow their unjust social privileges, Alcoff sees the attempt to repudiate white identity as itself a problem: "whites cannot completely disavow whiteness or distance themselves from their white identity. One's appearance of being white will still operate to confer privilege in numerous and significant ways" (215). Thinking that one has successfully disavowed whiteness when one hasn't is not only mistaken but counterproductive, licensing us to shirk responsibility to contribute to dismantling white supremacy. Those who disavow whiteness, Alcoff warns, "might consider a declaration that they are 'not white' as a sufficient solution to racism without the trouble of organizing or collective action. This position would then end up uncomfortably close to a color-blindness attitude that pretends ignorance about one's own white identity and refuses responsibility" (215).

This is what Alcoff calls *the whiteness problem*—"why maintain white identity at all, given that any group identity will be based on exclusion and an implicit superiority, and given that whiteness itself has been historically constituted as supremacist since its inception?" (2006, 221; also Bailey 1998). One way to address this is to remember, regarding whiteness and the value of identifying with histories and communities, that the histories of white supremacy and the white communities who accept their racial privilege unreflectively are not the *only* white histories and communities. Anti-racist whites must acknowledge their relationship to white racist histories and communities, Alcoff says, while also committing to keep "a newly awakened memory of the many white traitors to white privilege who have struggled to contribute to the building of an inclusive human community" (2006, 221).

Alcoff describes this white identity as a kind of double consciousness, inspired by but different from the double consciousness identified by W.E.B. Du Bois (1903). Here double consciousness means anti-racist whites acknowledging how white identity has figured into racial inequality and exploitation while also remembering the contributions made by anti-racist whites to dismantling white supremacy. Alcoff aims neither to let white people disassociate themselves from bad white histories and communities nor to allow white people to wallow in guilt-ridden stasis, as though an unavoidable white identity robs one of any and all capacity for anti-racist work. Histories of white anti-racism can also be histories with which white people identify, not instead of but alongside of histories of white privilege, ignorance, and exploitation. Identification with white anti-racism does not come automatically, to be sure. It must be earned—giving further impetus to white people genuinely committed to anti-racism to actually and persistently do something.

## FEMINIST ALLYSHIP: A RELATIONAL ACCOUNT

Alcoff's analysis of white anti-racism is worthwhile in its own right, but for present purposes, I want to emphasize two features that extend fruitfully to the question of feminist masculinity. The first point is her insistence that socially privileged identity and group membership are not easily disavowed: not only will disavowal be difficult for the person himself given a lifetime of privilege, but the world will continue to confer privilege in many subtle, pervasive ways regardless of one's disavowals. In this way privilege is, as Marilyn Frye put it, "an odd sort of self-regenerative thing which, once you've got it, cannot be simply shucked off like a too-warm jacket" (1992, 29).

The second complementary point is that allyship against oppression can be constitutive of anti-racist whiteness, through contributions to justice and an abiding sense of how such contributions fit into anti-racist white histories and communities. This point dovetails with Harry Brod's (1998, 210) critique of Stoltenberg's (1989, 1993) rejection of manhood: "what is lacking is precisely the standpoint from which to practice a transformative politics that being profeminist as men provides. One is left with only an ungendered individual moral identity, rather than a gendered collective political identity that I believe is essential for sustained, effective political action." Judith Newton similarly emphasizes the importance of "the pleasures of collectivity" (2002, 183) available to men which can help sustain their progressive political activities.

In this spirit, the sort of reclaimed feminist masculinity I have in mind frames masculinity in political, gendered, and relational terms. Specifically, I submit that allyship enables a viable open-ended normative model for feminist masculinity distinct from androgyny (although friendly to it) and grounded in feminist values. To start, let us describe an ally as one who supports and works alongside another in a shared project or end (Gibson 2014, 200; Blankschaen 2016, 9; Smith and Johnson 2020, 7). For present purposes, I would note three features of allyship relevant to feminist masculinity. The first is that a good ally neither dominates nor takes over a shared project. As bell hooks reminds us, the goal is one of cooperation rather than domination (hooks 2004, 117; Smith and Johnson 2020, 8). This leads to our second point: the project is shared (Edwards 2006), meaning that an ally working with others values the project relationally. It is not merely that their interests happen to converge, but rather, they value the project at least in part *because* these others value it as well—allyship is an invested relationship (Sullivan-Clarke 2020b, 32). The third point is that an ally is in some significant sense in coalition with others (Reagon 1983): an alliance is a relationship involving allied parties who are nonidentical in a relevant way rather than, as Raewyn Connell aptly puts it, "mobilization of one group around its common interest" (2005, 205). No two parties are wholly identical, of course: the point is that differences between or among allies are themselves relevant to their participation and their contributions to be made in the shared project, and thus relevant to their relationship being one of allies working together in coalition.

This way of thinking about allyship embraces differences among allies as a source of collective strength rather than an obstacle to overcome. This echoes Audre Lorde's (1984, 110) argument in "The Master's Tools Will Never Dismantle the Master's House," that differences among women are not to be feared or ignored, and if solidarity is based only on what all women have in common, then women of color will only continue to be marginalized and excluded from mainstream feminist analyses and actions. My hope is that the account of feminist allyship masculinity to be articulated in the rest of this book does justice to Lorde's insight. One notable feature of my approach here is that while I underline the importance of difference, I do not follow many sociologists and men's studies scholars who draw a bright line between allies and other members of social movements. Daniel Myers for example differentiates between *beneficiaries* and *allies*, where the former are "rank-and-file activists who hail from the population that would expect or wish to benefit from the movement's activities," and the latter are "movement adherents who are not direct beneficiaries of the movements they support and do not have an expectation of such benefits" (2008, 167).

It can indeed be useful to distinguish between those who benefit from a social movement and those who do not, but feminist allyship as I understand it does not neatly track that distinction. As with hooks' observation that it can be true that patriarchy both oppresses women and harms men too, I would not want to assume that men do not and cannot benefit from emancipatory feminism, nor that allies more generally do not and cannot benefit from the social movements in which they participate (hooks 1984, 73; Pease 2000, 37). "One of the things holding men back from being better allies," argues Kimberly Doyle, "is they don't often understand what they have to gain from being an ally" (Smith and Johnson 2020, 9). To say that men can benefit from gender justice is not to presume that men benefit as much or in the same way as their allies, just as we can recognize that all women and gender non-binary people do not benefit in exactly the same way from gender justice either. I would not want to assert that men by definition cannot be feminist allies to one another nor that women or non-binary people cannot also be feminist allies to differently situated others with whom they work in coalition across difference. For Emma Dabiri (2021, 85–86), the dubious distinction between allies and beneficiaries is one reason why she urges moving from allyship to building coalitions around our shared interests. When the concept is decoupled from beneficence, however, we do not have to choose between allyship and coalition. We can recognize that working together in coalition across difference is itself at the heart of ally relationships.

Related to the *non-beneficiary* conception is what we might call a *dominant group membership* conception of allyship, such that allies are by definition dominant group members seeking to end prejudice in their own lives, relinquish their privilege, and foster institutional and cultural change (Brown and Ostrove 2013). While many contemporary discussions of allies and allyship start from this sort of definition (cf. Gibson 2014; Brown 2015; McKinnon 2017; Bourke 2020; Radke et al. 2020), I share Andrea Sullivan-Clarke's concern that it "renders the contributions from individuals from outside the dominant social group invisible" (2020b, 34). Sullivan-Clarke identifies Veterans Stand with Standing Rock (VSSR) and Black Lives Matter (#BLM) as two groups whose actions against the Dakota Access Pipeline incursion on Standing Rock tribal lands made them not only active bystanders but committed allies to Indigenous water protectors there:

> Once one considered the examples of VSSR and #BLM, it becomes apparent that the definition of allyship proposed by Ostrove and Brown fails to sufficiently address the needs of colonized people. The VSSR and #BLM allies at Standing Rock were not necessarily from privileged groups, and it is difficult to locate the privilege they are relinquishing so that others may be treated humanely. (2020a, 183)

Sullivan-Clarke sees critical roles for both allies and active bystanders in Indigenous environmental justice but resists the idea that the contributions of members of non-dominant groups are limited to latter category. "An active bystander steps in as the need arises and may intervene in real time" (2020a, 181); while this is indeed valuable to the goals of social justice, it also means that "active bystanders are not committed to act beyond the moment and once completed, it seems their work is done" (2020b, 32). The actions of VSSR and #BLM members at Standing Rock substantiated a more lasting, epistemically and affectively committed relationship to Indigenous water protectors, which Sullivan Clarke identifies as working toward decolonial allyship. "It is a relationship that is not temporary, but reflects an investment in the flourishing of both participants" (2020b, 36). To insist that only members of dominant groups can act as allies is, she says, to continue to understand allyship in colonial terms.

A proponent of the dominant group membership conception of allies and allyship might remind us that individuals can be members of dominant groups in one respect but not another, given the multiple systems of oppression predicated on race, class, colonialism, gender, sexuality, religion, and other aspects of human social identities. Thus members from different non-dominant groups still could be allies to one another provided that they also hold membership in a dominant group: for example, that Black men could be allies to white women in virtue of their gender while white women could be allies to Black men in virtue of their race. I worry however, that as a general rule this conception only works by presuming a narrowly additive conception of social oppression that intersectional feminist theorists take pains to dispel (Spelman 1988; Crenshaw 1989; Taiwo 2018). Intersectionality affirms not only that people are oppressed in different ways but that the axes of oppression *intersect* in messy, complicated, not so easily disentangled ways. To insist that Black men can be allies for white women only in virtue of their gender would be to presume that Black men experience oppression only ever in virtue of their identities as Black and never in virtue of their identities as Black men specifically. To insist that white women can be allies for Black men only in virtue of their race would similarly presume that white women experience oppression only ever in virtue of their identities as women and never in virtue of their identities as white women more specifically. One feature of the relational approach to allyship that I take here is that it allows for and is indeed grounded in recognition of social differences between and among allied parties, but does so without assuming that allyship practices can only be performed when one falls on the non-beneficiary or dominant-group side of a coalition. While this way of conceiving allyship may not align with how it tends to be framed in contemporary sociological and popular discussions, it is not especially new either. In a special issue of the feminist journal *Sinister Wisdom*, for example, Gloria Anzaldúa (1994), Andrea Calderón (1994), and other contributors speak about allyship in relationally mutual terms, where different communities of color and differently positioned women can be allies for one another. As Lisa Rudman (1994) puts it, "I think allies recognize differences and connections between us and ask, how are we going to function with each other?"

To make sense of feminist allyship in particular, let us consider feminism broadly construed. Susan Sherwin identifies several commitments common to a wide range of feminist theories:

> a recognition that women are in a subordinate position in society, that oppression is a form of injustice and hence intolerable, that there are further forms of oppression in addition to gender oppression (and that there are women victimized by each of these forms of oppression), that it is possible to change society in ways that could eliminate oppression, and that it is a goal of feminism to pursue the changes necessary to accomplish this. (1989, 70)

One might add further commitments to these, to be sure, commitments central to and distinctive of various approaches to feminism. But starting here, we can say at least that *feminists* share these recognitions and contribute to pursuing such changes. Applying our general conception of allyship, we can further say that *feminist allies* come to such feminist recognitions and pursue such work alongside varied others, appreciating that others bring their own perspectives and experiences to bear on the work and ideas. Feminist allies make complementary contributions without subsuming, appropriating, erasing, or preventing others' recognitions or their contributions. *Feminist allyship masculinity*, then, recognizes how gender norms and configurations of masculinity and femininity undergird social oppression, recognizes how those of us who are men both uphold oppressive systems and also can contribute to dismantling them, and achieves such recognitions and makes such contributions to undoing oppression in ways that are both similar to and different from our feminist allies, such differences owing to what differentiates our positionalities with regard to this work.

Sally Haslanger (2000, 42) reminds us that being a man under patriarchy is at least in part about how one is interpreted by others (and by oneself) as occupying a social position of male privilege. Manhood is fungible, gender fluidity is possible, yet as with Alcoff's observation about antiracist whiteness, attempting to disavow manhood to repudiate patriarchy is no guarantee as long as the world "will still operate to confer privilege in numerous and significant ways" (2006, 213). This is of course not to deny the right of trans women and men to affirm their respective identities as women and men against presumptive social categorization. Men seeking to distance themselves from masculinity in order to deny their gender privilege are in a rather different position, one in which repudiation of manhood assuages guilt and shame and encourages the tempting conclusion that doing this is sufficient to wash one's hands of what Connell calls the "patriarchal dividend" (2005, 79). What men can do instead of attempting to purge ourselves of manhood is to exercise more significant and deliberate control over how we respond to privilege and patriarchy in ways that are consistent with and grounded in feminist values.

Masculinities, Connell and Messerschmidt (2005, 836) argue, are "configurations of practice." We can regard men's feminist allyship practices as constitutive of normative feminist masculinity such that the norms of feminist allyship give meaning to better ways of being men, ways that are distinct, constructive, and intersectional. Feminist masculinity so understood involves something akin to the awareness Alcoff describes—in this case, feminist men recognizing how men benefit from and are complicit in gender oppression while recognizing the meaningful contributions to undoing oppression that men have made historically and can make going forward. (I would make no assertion of masculine double consciousness, however, as I do not mean to suggest anything akin to what Du Bois describes as the pervasive lived experience of oppressed peoples.) Contrary to Michael Salter's (2019) warning that contemporary criticisms of toxic masculinity risk reifying a commitment to a singular, real masculinity, some "fixed set of identities and attributes," allyship masculinity is compatible with Connell's recognition of masculinity as a product of arrangements, behaviors, and relationships. Feminist allyship masculinity is concerned not so much with finding an authentic manhood within each of us individually as it is with our recognition and participation in the ongoing creation of feminist configurations of practice.

Allyship has a social-epistemic dimension. Consider for example the idea of a progressive male standpoint grounded in critical reflection upon one's own experiences as a man alongside mindful attention to women's experiences as they share them (May 1998, 135; Pease 2000, 5–6). Achieving and maintaining this standpoint takes work, dedication, self-scrutiny, and sincere willingness to listen humbly. Drawing upon both men's and women's experiences of a gendered world, May's progressive man does so as a faithful ally standing in different relation to women's experiences than they do themselves. Indeed, May's own account may be understood reflexively, as he strives to meet his own standard for a progressive male standpoint, drawing upon Bat-Ami Bar On, Sandra Harding, and others while testifying to his own particular perspective and gendered experiences (May 1998; Alcoff and Potter 1993).

In allyship masculinity, we can find resolution to the paradox of feminist pride in manhood aptly articulated by Richard Schmitt (2001, 399): "since we are not profeminists with unspecified gender but specifically profeminist men, we struggle in fact against ourselves, against what most persons in our society expect us to be, and against what we were raised to be." Schmitt realizes that self-hatred while tempting cannot enable long-term contributions to feminist progress; yet he also feels that a call for pride in manhood "carries with it overtones of the old patriarchy with its distinctions between the natures of men and women" (399). In response, Harry Brod stresses that "men having a positive sense of themselves and pride in themselves as men, is first and foremost part of a political project, part of an effort to encourage and empower men to take collective action against sexism" (2001, 405). While I can sympathize with Schmitt's apprehension, I think Brod is correct to pull us away from pride in terms of some essential gender difference and toward pride in terms of our contributions to collective action. If we acknowledge how men's specific positions in patriarchal systems constrain and enable our relationships and contributions to social justice, we may better appreciate that the pride available to men as feminist allies is not pride in an essential male nature but pride in doing the work one can as a feminist man.

## Ally Trouble?

The idea, then, is to understand men's feminist allyship as non-essentialist practices of normative masculinity not only compatible with feminist values but grounded in them. Allyship masculinity shares with androgyny an opposition to traditional gender norms and oppressive power structures; the various behaviors and activities identified here as normatively masculine do not concern how we should dress, hold our bodies, pitch our voices, or numerous other traditionally gendered things. Instead, this reclamation of normative feminist masculinity is akin to Alcoff's counsel to anti-racist whites to do the work necessary to become contributing members of anti-racist white communities and histories. Doing the work of feminist allyship masculinity so understood means contributing meaningfully to feminist work while being mindful of how our gendered privileges, expectations, ignorance, and knowledge as men situate our relationships and our contributions to this work in coalition with differently situated allies.

One might wonder what sort of account of normative feminist femininity is supposed to follow then from this account of normative feminist masculinity. My aim here is to make sense of feminist masculinity for its own sake, not to position masculinity as a default category with straightforward isomorphic implications for other gender categories. I would resist drawing conclusions from the present discussion for what feminist femininity should look like, or even whether this would be a good way to go about thinking of things. Men's masculinities certainly are not the only existing or possible masculinities and normative masculinity is not the only conception of masculinity worth recognizing and considering (Connell 2005, 67–71). Norms of feminist allyship masculinity need not negate or limit performances of female masculinity nor performances of masculinity by non-binary people. As Jack Halberstam says, "it is crucial to recognize that masculinity does not belong to men, has not been produced only by men, and does not properly express male heterosexuality …it is inaccurate and indeed regressive to make masculinity into a general term of behavior associated with males" (1998, 241).[1]

---

[1] While feminist allyship as a viable normative masculinity for men and boys is not proposed as a general categorical characterization that would preclude female, non-binary, genderqueer, or other masculinities, whether Halberstam would endorse this proposal is a separate question, one I cannot presume to answer.

Whatever else it may have to contribute, the concept of allyship masculinity is not meant to be a generalized descriptive account of male behavior. To paraphrase Ruth Abbey (2019, 12), men's performances of allyship masculinity are more contingent than tautological. There are many ways that people are and can be masculine, and allyship masculinity would not subsume or replace them all. Its aspirations are more limited: not a general account of masculinity but more specifically a normative framework for men compatible with and grounded in feminist values and practices. While I hope readers find allyship to be a compelling, constructive basis for a feminist alternative to both feminist androgyny and patriarchal masculinity, I would not presume to claim that it is the only such alternative pathway available.[2]

In looking to feminist allyship practices as giving meaning to normative feminist masculinity, I do not mean to present allyship as something simple or uncontested. Some theorists and activists see allies and allyship as playing vital roles in social justice movements (Bishop 2002; Kivel 2011; Kivel 2013; Ravarino 2013; Drury and Kaiser 2014; Bridges and Mather 2015; Blankschaen 2016; Sullivan-Clarke 2020a). Others are more critical, particularly when it comes to men, white, straight, cisgender, and upper-class people describing themselves as allies (McKenzie 2014; Anderson and Accomando 2016; McKinnon 2017; Bourke 2020; Pugh 2020; Hesford 2021). "Don't call yourself an ally," Smith and Johnson (2020, 83) caution. "You are an ally for a woman when she calls you an ally and never before." Ally self-ascriptions raise suspicion because they are further evidence of privileged persons' misplaced priorities, focused more on glorification and public performance than doing the work of undoing oppressive structures. "Allyship is not supposed to look like this, folks," Mia McKenzie (2014, 180) writes. "It's supposed to be a way of living your life that doesn't reinforce the same oppressive behaviors you're claiming to be against." Kurt Blankschaen (2016, 13) agrees with McKenzie's critique of bad allies, though he still thinks the concept of allyship is worth saving. If nothing else, critics and proponents can agree that "ally" is better understood as a verb rather than a noun, a sustained activity rather than a badge of honor.

---

[2] On the possibility of Deleuzian minoritarian feminism and masculinity, for example, see Goulimari (1999), Stark (2017), McDonald (2018), and Hickey-Moody (2019). My thanks to an anonymous reviewer for pressing this point.

Indeed, the trouble is not limited to self-appointed "allies" but also includes contemporary social institutions that hand out and even sell ally badges, what Indigenous Action Media calls the "ally industrial complex" (2014). When allyship is commodified, its market depends on oppression as a persisting reality and those individuals and entities selling ally certification have conflicts between their driving profit motives and their ostensibly primary motivation to end oppression. Meanwhile those given the external validation of ally certification may exhibit the same sorts of complacency and overconfidence as self-ascribed allies do. They may feel that no further action is required once awarded the ally label (Bourke 2020) or feel licensed to correct and gaslight oppressed people on what "really" happened to them (McKinnon 2017). "A person's behavior seems permitted given their status as an ally, but it really seems that how they perform for an oppressed group should be the focus" Sullivan-Clarke (2020a, 41) notes. As Rhian Waters puts it, our goal should be fostering "acts of allyhood" (2010, 2) more than ally attributions.

For these reasons I have sought to articulate allyship masculinity in terms of feminist practices and projects rather than self-ascriptions or institutional certifications. My hope is that maintaining focus on the practices that ground normative masculinity can avoid the self-congratulatory excess of allies and allyship culture. It is not enough for men to view or describe themselves as feminist allies in order to live up to allyship masculinity norms, any more than would be enough to view or describe oneself as trustworthy or generous in order to live up to norms of trust or generosity. It is similarly not enough to complete an official ally training to be a good ally any more than it would be enough to complete an ethics training to make ethical choices, develop a virtuous character, or stand in morally healthy relationships. So understood, the extent to which men individually and collectively are practicing allyship masculinity effectively will be because of what we have done and what we are doing, not by our titles or what we like to call ourselves.

This is not to say engaging in allyship practices is an always unqualified good. For one thing, it might be presumptive to regard certain social justice projects *as* shared projects. This is among Catherine Pugh's reasons for skepticism about ally talk when it comes to white supremacy and the systematic perpetuation of violence against Black people. "Racism is not mine, it's yours, and it's not called 'help' when it's your mess we're cleaning," Pugh argues (2020). Even if we do not see allies in terms of auxiliary or secondary helpers, the point remains—dismantling white supremacy should be recognized as white people's responsibility, rather than a responsibility they share with its victims. Furthermore, even when a project genuinely is shared, taking allyship as a relationship seriously means taking the conditions of healthy, trustful relationality seriously too. If I have not done the work needed for you to trust me as a potential ally, it could be not only ineffective but disrespectful for me to proceed as if that relational foundation were already in place. Relatedly, if I am unwilling to acknowledge prior or persisting injustices and to affirm your core social, ethical, epistemic, and even metaphysical commitments, I should not presume to have built the credibility I need to engage collaboratively in allyship practices toward the more advanced goals we share for social justice. The allyship practices that *are* open to me at this earlier stage are these more basic reparative acts of acknowledgment and affirmation, which I cannot rush past as uncomfortable or inconvenient. This is the difference that Sullivan-Clarke sees between merely putative allies and genuinely decolonial allies at Standing Rock (2020b, 36–38). The latter not only act in support of Indigenous water protectors but affirm Indigenous sovereignty and self-determination, listen, and learn their histories—which includes their own (frequently ignored) histories and relationships to colonialization and settler privilege (see also Whyte 2018).

One concern about emphasizing the ways that men as feminist allies can help to make positive contributions to gender equity is that it risks erasing men's complicity with and responsibility for perpetration of past and persisting violence against women and other forms of gender oppression. Men have vital roles to play in undoing patriarchy, not just because we are well positioned to do so but because we benefit from and contribute to it. We know the perpetrators of misogyny and of gender injustice more generally, because oftentimes we ourselves are those perpetrators. This is a concern raised by the authors and multiple interviewees in Messner, Greenberg, and Peretz's book *Some Men*, on their ambivalence toward the growing popularity and influence of active bystander programs (2015, 121). Whether on college campuses, football teams, in the military, or elsewhere, Jackson Katz's Mentors in Violence Prevention (MVP) Program and similar initiatives teach men to become active bystanders who step in to prevent or stop violence against women (Messner 2016, 62–64; Katz 2019, 277–310). What often becomes sidelined in these trainings, however, is the need to acknowledge and reckon with men as perpetrators of sexual assault and other forms of gender violence. In the rhetoric and role-playing of bystander trainings, it is inevitably *other* men who assault women, while *we* either passively let it happen or actively intervene as good men (Messner et al. 2015, 123).

This eliding of men's perpetration of injustice extends beyond violence prevention programs to patriarchal systems and institutions and misogyny experienced by women and non-binary people throughout their lives. The point is not that men's complicity and perpetrations of gender injustice make us forever unfit for feminist allyship—although the more and more we fail to acknowledge these injustices and work to make things right, the less and less our potential allies have reason to trust us. Feminist allyship masculinity is constituted by doing the reparative work to rebuild what has been damaged or destroyed by our own and other men's perpetrations of gender oppression (Walker 2010, 2015). It means being accountable to our allies not only for the ways that we contribute to collective feminist projects, and not only for our bouts of bystander paralysis and other failures to act, but also for what we have done wrong, what we are still doing wrong now, and what we will do wrong in the future (Smith and Johnson 2020, 112; Jha 2021, 172).

"The biggest risk in forming alliances is betrayal," argues Gloria Anzaldúa (1994, 50). Injuries inflicted by one's allies are especially painful not despite but because of the relational vulnerability involved. Uma Narayan (1988, 35) explains:

> The disadvantaged cannot fail to realize that being hurt by the insensitivity of members of the advantaged groups they endeavor to work with and care about, is often more difficult to deal with emotionally than being hurt by the deliberate malice of members of advantaged groups they expect no better of. Here, members of disadvantaged groups render themselves vulnerable because they accept the existence of good will… and have good reason to expect that they will, often enough, be hurt, good will not withstanding.

Feminist allyship as collaboration across gender and other social differences requires trust across gender and other social differences. As Annette Baier (1986) reminds us, trust is a valuable, fragile thing: difficult to build and maintain, and even harder to rebuild once betrayed.

## ALLYSHIP AND INTERSECTIONALITY

In the previous chapter I raised concerns about the accounts of masculinity offered by bell hooks, Michael Kimmel, and others, that the things they see as constitutive of masculinity are embodied and expressed equally well by women and men. It is fair to ask, then, whether feminist allyship as a model for masculinity invites a similar critique. Does my own approach attribute something to men that is not distinctive of them? Women too act in contribution to feminist work, after all, mindful of how their sexually marked privileges affect how they understand this work. Men and women both can accrue gender privileges, some might argue, if and when they satisfy socially prescribed (heterosexist, classist, racist, etc.) norms. If gender privilege is not distinctive of what it means to be a man within a patriarchal society, does an allyship model of feminist masculinity face the same sort of problem raised for hooks, Kimmel, and others in the previous chapter?

I take this as a welcome challenge for allyship masculinities built around the recognition that, as men, our relationship to patriarchy is distinctively different than women and non-binary people, and our contributions to feminist work are sometimes distinctively different than our allies. It is true that sexuality, race, and other social categories undeniably affect how and when men are accorded gender privilege; it is also fair to say, at least in some sense, that women are rewarded if and when they conform to patriarchal requirements. Yet the ways in which men and women are accorded gender-based privileges are distinctively different, and the norms of men's feminist allyship practices direct us to mind these differences in our gender privileges as we reflect, listen, speak, and act accordingly.

The ways in which different men are accorded gender privilege can also be different, of course. Intersectional feminist theorists (Spelman 1988; Crenshaw 1989; Crenshaw 1991; Collins and Bilge 2016) explain that the patriarchal oppression of women does not mean that all women experience patriarchy in exactly the same way. This does not mean only some women are truly oppressed, of course, nor does it mean that because their experiences of oppression are not identical then women across race and class identities have no basis for solidarity. The relevant intersectional insight here is that oppression works in a more complex fashion: sexism in practice is not isolated from racism, classism, homophobia, or other axes of oppression as these things are not isolated from each other either. An analogous point holds for how different men experience patriarchy. Consider Peggy McIntosh's familiar image of a knapsack of privileges, a collection of social privileges large and small that each man carries around with him, always there even when taken for granted by the recipient himself (McIntosh 1988; see also Mutua 2012). Indeed, the ability to take these privileges for granted is itself a significant kind of privilege. Inside different knapsacks are some but not all of the same things; not all men across all social categories are accorded the same gender privileges manifested in the same way. So one upshot of an intersectional approach to male privilege is the reminder that as men strive to be trustworthy allies to women and non-binary people, so too can differently positioned men work to be trustworthy allies to each other. The coalition among allies may be diverse indeed.

What does an intersectional approach mean for a feminist model of normative masculinity? It complicates things in welcome and constructive ways. Men must work to be better feminist allies to women by recognizing the diversity among women's identities and experiences, remembering that allyship with women necessarily bridges multiple dimensions of social power and difference. Men and women must work to be better allies to non-binary people, remembering also that those who live outside the gender binary of course have considerable differences among themselves too, and that given their different positions within patriarchy, men and women have different norms to fulfill and contributions to make as allies to non-binary people. Men likewise can be better allies to other men, recognizing the diversity among their wide-ranging identities and experiences and appreciating how trustworthy allyship among men requires bridging differences too.

What is it, then, that makes various men's feminist allyship practices *masculine*, something that differentiates them from feminist women and non-binary people? It is obviously not that only men can be allies. Nor is it that all men should do the same things in their capacity as feminist allies. What is distinctive of men's feminist allyship practices, and what makes them constitutive of a distinct kind of normative feminist masculinity, is that they are informed by and grounded in men's experiences of and positionings within patriarchal systems as men. These are not always the same experiences, to be sure, but the fact that the people in question are men and not otherwise is significant for how patriarchy affects them, and so also significant for how they should contribute to its destruction.

When I am doing my part as best as I am able, my practices of feminist allyship masculinity overlap with and also differ from how feminist allyship masculinity is practiced by other similarly and differently positioned men. For this reason, we might do well to think of normative feminist masculinities, pluralized, recognizing a panoply of gender privileges and expectations accorded to men, pluralized, living within patriarchal systems. And just as feminist advocates of androgyny see its application not only to individual men and women but also to social systems and institutions, we can envision, (re)build, and celebrate histories, communities, cultures, and institutions rooted in men's feminist allyship (see for example Kimmel and Mosmiller 1992; Guy-Sheftall 2006; Nall 2010). Among the distinct tasks for men striving to fulfill norms of feminist allyship masculinities are to reflect on and discuss the particular ways in which each of us experience gender privileges and expectations as men, so as to develop a better understanding of our particular place in feminist politics and to make more apt contributions to feminist projects accordingly.

## References

Abbey, Ruth, and Masculinity. 2019. In *The Wollstonecraftian Mind*, ed. Sandrine Berges, Eileen Hunt Botting, and Alan Coffee, 365–377. New York: Routledge.

Alcoff, Linda Martín. 2006. *Visible Identities: Race, Gender, and the Self*. Oxford: Oxford University Press.

Alcoff, Linda, and Elizabeth Potter, eds. 1993. *Feminist Epistemologies*. New York: Routledge.

Anderson, Kristin J, and Christina Hsu Accomando. 2016. The Pitfalls of Allyship Performance: Why Coalition Work Is More Effective than Ally Theater. *Psychology Today*, August 10.

Anzaldúa, Gloria. 1994. Interview with Jamie Lee Evans. *Sinister Wisdom* 52: 47–52.

Baier, Annette. 1986. Trust and Anti-Trust. *Ethics* 96 (2): 231–260.

Bailey, Allison. 1998. Locating Traitorous Identities: Toward a View of Privilege-Cognizant White Identity. *Hypatia* 13 (3): 27–42.

Bishop, Anne. 2002. *Becoming an Ally*. London: Zed Books.

Blankschaen, Kurt. 2016. Allied Identities. *Feminist Philosophy Quarterly* 2 (2).

Bourke, Brian. 2020. Leaving Behind the Rhetoric of Allyship. *Whiteness and Education* 5 (2): 179–194.

Bridges, Christopher Edward, and Peter Mather. 2015. Joining the Struggle: White Men as Social Justice Allies. *Journal of College and Character* 16 (3): 155–168.

Brod, Harry. 1998. To Be a Man, or Not to Be a Man—That Is the Feminist Question. In *Men Doing Feminism*, ed. Tom Digby. New York: Routledge.
———. 2001. Male Pride and Antisexism. *Men and Masculinities* 3 (4): 405–410.
Brown, Kendrick. 2015. Perceiving Allies from the Perspective of Non-dominant Group Members: Comparisons to Friends and Activists. *Current Psychology* 34: 713–722.
Brown, Kendrick, and Joan Ostrove. 2013. What Does It Mean to Be an Ally? The Perception of Allies from the Perspective of People of Color. *Journal of Applied Social Psychology* 43 (11): 2211–2222.
Calderón, Andrea. 1994. Interview with Jamie Lee Evans. *Sinister Wisdom* 52: 13–16.
Collins, Patricia Hill, and Sirma Bilge. 2016. *Intersectionality*. Malden, MA: Polity Press.
Connell, Raewyn. 2005. *Masculinities*. Berkeley: University of California Press.
Connell, Raewyn, and James Messerschmidt. 2005. Hegemonic Masculinity. *Gender and Society* 19 (6): 829–859.
Crenshaw, Kimberle. 1989. Demarginalizing the Intersection of Race and Sex. *University of Chicago Law Forum* 139.
———. 1991. Mapping the Margins: Intersectionality, Identity Politics, and Violence against Women of Color. *Stanford Law Review* 43: 1241.
Dabiri, Emma. 2021. *What White People Can Do Next*. New York: Harper.
Drury, Benjami J., and Cheryl R. Kaiser. 2014. Allies against Sexism: The Role of Men in Confronting Sexism. *Journal of Social Issues* 70 (4): 637–652.
Du Bois, W.E.B. 1903. *The Souls of Black Folk*. Chicago: A.C. McClurg.
Edwards, K. 2006. Aspiring Social Justice Ally Identity Development: A Conceptual Model. *NASPA Journal* 43 (4): 39–60.
Frye, Marilyn. 1992. *Willful Virgin: Essays in Feminism*. Boston: The Crossing Press.
Gibson, Priscilla Ann. 2014. Extending the Ally Model of Social Justice to Social Work Pedagogy. *Journal of Teaching in Social Work* 34 (2): 199–214.
Goulimari, Pelagia. 1999. A Minoritarian Feminism? Things to Do with Deleuze and Guattari. *Hypatia* 14 (2): 97–120.
Guy-Sheftall, Beverly. 2006. Remembering our Feminist Forefathers. In *Progressive Black Masculinities*, ed. D. Athena, 43–54. Mutua. New York: Routledge.
Halberstam, Jack. 1998. *Female Masculinity*. Durham: Duke University Press.
Haslanger, Sally. 2000. Gender and Race: (What) Are They? (What) Do We Want Them to Be? *Nous* 34 (1): 31–55.
Hesford, Wendy. 2021. Reading the Signs: Performative White Allyship. *Quarterly Journal of Speech* 107 (2): 239–244.
Hickey-Moody, Anna. 2019. *Deleuze and Masculinity*. Palgrave Macmillan.
hooks, bell. 1984. *Feminist Theory: From Margin to Center*. Boston: South End.
———. 2004. *The Will to Change: Men, Masculinity, and Love*. New York: Atria Books.

Indigenous Action Media. 2014. Accomplices not Allies: Abolishing the Ally Industrial Complex. https://www.indigenousaction.org/accomplices-not-allies-abolishing-the-ally-industrial-complex/.

Jha, Sonora. 2021. *How to Raise a Feminist Son*. Seattle: Sasquatch.

Katz, Jackson. (2006) 2019. *The Macho Paradox: Why Some Men Hurt Women and How All Men Can Help*. Naperville: Sourcebooks.

Kimmel, Michael, and Thomas Mosmiller. 1992. *Against the Tide: Pro-feminist Men in the United States, 1776–1990*. Boston: Beacon Press.

Kivel, Paul. 2011. *Uprooting Racism: How White People Can Work for Racial Justice*. New Society Publishers.

———. 2013. *Living in the Shadow of the Cross: Understanding and Resisting the Power and Privilege of Christian Hegemony*. New Society Publishers.

Lorde, Audre. (1984) 2007. *Sister Outsider: Essays and Speeches*. Berkeley: Crossing Press.

May, Larry. 1998. *Masculinity and Morality*. Ithaca: Cornell University Press.

McDonald, Terrance. 2018. Conceptualizing an Ethology of Masculinities. *Men and Masculinities* 21 (1): 56–71.

McIntosh, Peggy. 1988. *White Privilege and Male Privilege*. Wellesley College: Center for Research on Women.

McKenzie, Mia. 2014. *Black Girl Dangerous: On Race, Queerness, Class and Gender*. Oakland: BGD Press.

McKinnon, Rachel. 2017. Gaslighting as Epistemic Injustice. In *Routledge Handbook of Epistemic Injustice*, ed. Ian James Kidd Gaile Pohlhaus Jr. and Jose Medina, 167–174. Oxford: Routledge.

Messner, Michael. 2016. Bad Men, Good Men, Bystanders. *Gender & Society* 30 (1): 57–66.

Messner, Michael, Max Greenberg, and Tal Peretz. 2015. *Some Men: Feminist Allies and the Movement to End Violence against Women*. Oxford University Press.

Mutua, Athena D. 2012. Multidimensionality is to Masculinities What Intersectionality is to Feminism. *Nevada Law Journal* 13: 341–367.

Myers, Daniel J. 2008. Ally Identity: The Politically Gay. In *Identity Work in Social Movements*, ed. Jo Reger, Daniel J. Myers, and Rachel L. Einwohner, 167–187. Minneapolis: University of Minnesota Press.

Nall, Jeff. 2010. Exhuming the History of Feminist Masculinity. *Culture, Society & Masculinity* 2 (1): 42.

Narayan, Uma. 1988. Working Together Across Difference: Some Considerations of Emotions and Political Practice. *Hypatia* 3 (2): 31–47.

Newton, Judith. 2002. Masculinity Studies: The Longed-for Profeminist Movement for Academic Men? In *Masculinity Studies and Feminist Theory*, ed. Judith K. Garner, 176–192. New York: Columbia University Press.

Pease, Bob. 2000. *Recreating Men: Postmodern Masculinity Politics*. Los Angeles: Sage.

Pugh, Catherine. 2020. There is No Such Thing as a 'White Ally'. *Human Parts*, June 15. Online. https://humanparts.medium.com/there-is-no-such-thing-as-a-white-ally-469bb82799f2.
Radke, Helena R.M., Maja Kutlaca, Birte Siem, Stephen C. Wright, and Julia C. Becker. 2020. Beyond Allyship: Motivations for Advantaged Group Members to Engage in Action for Disadvantaged Groups. *Personality and Social Psychology Review* 24 (4): 291–315.
Ravarino, Jonathan. 2013. Being a Social Justice Ally. In *Men Speak Out*, ed. Shiva Tarrant, 174–181. New York: Routledge.
Reagon, Bernice Johnson. 1983. Coalition Politics: Turning the Century. In *Home Girls: A Black Feminist Anthology*, ed. Barbara Smith. New York: Kitchen Table Press.
Rudman, Lisa. 1994. Interview with Jamie Lee Evans. *Sinister Wisdom* 52: 21–25.
Salter, Michael. 2019. The Problem with a Fight Against Toxic Masculinity. *The Atlantic*, Feb 27.
Schmitt, Richard. 2001. Proud to Be a Man? *Men and Masculinities* 3 (4): 393–404.
Sherwin, Susan. 1989. Feminism and Medical Ethics. *Hypatia* 4 (2): 57–72.
Smith, David G., and W. Brad Johnson. 2020. *Good Guys: How Men Can Be Better Allies for Women in the Workplace*. Boston, MA: Harvard Business Review Press.
Spelman, Elizabeth. 1988. *Inessential Woman: Problems of Exclusion in Feminist Thought*. Boston: Beacon Press.
Stark, Hannah. 2017. *Feminist Theory after Deleuze*. London: Bloomsbury Academic.
Stoltenberg, John. 1989. *Refusing to be a Man*. London: University College London Press.
———. 1993. *The End of Manhood: A Book for Men of Conscience*. London: Dutton.
Sullivan-Clarke, Andrea. 2020a. Decolonizing 'Allyship' for Indian Country: Lessons from #NODAPL. *Hypatia* 35: 178–189.
———. 2020b. Empowering Relations: An Indigenous Understanding of Allyship in North American. *Journal of World Philosophies* 5: 30–42.
Taiwo, Olufemi. 2018. *The Man Not* and the Dilemmas of Intersectionality. *APA Newsletter on Philosophy and the Black Experience* 17 (2): 6–10.
Walker, Margaret Urban. 2010. *What is Reparative Justice?* Milwaukee: Marquette University Press.
———. 2015. Making Reparations Possible: Theorizing Reparative Justice. In *Theorizing Transitional Justice*, ed. Claudio Corradetti, Nir Eisikovits, and Jack V. Rotondi, 211–225. London: Ashgate.
Waters, Rhian. 2010. Understanding Allyship as a Developmental Process. *About Campus* 15 (5): 2–8.
Whyte, Kyle. 2018. White Allies, Let's be Honest about Decolonization. *Yes! Magazine,* April 3.

**Open Access**  This chapter is licensed under the terms of the Creative Commons Attribution 4.0 International License (http://creativecommons.org/licenses/by/4.0/), which permits use, sharing, adaptation, distribution and reproduction in any medium or format, as long as you give appropriate credit to the original author(s) and the source, provide a link to the Creative Commons licence and indicate if changes were made.

The images or other third party material in this chapter are included in the chapter's Creative Commons licence, unless indicated otherwise in a credit line to the material. If material is not included in the chapter's Creative Commons licence and your intended use is not permitted by statutory regulation or exceeds the permitted use, you will need to obtain permission directly from the copyright holder.

CHAPTER 6

# Allyship Masculinities in the Unjust Meantime

**Abstract** This chapter explores the intersectional potential of and challenges for feminist allyship masculinities in social context. What does it mean for allyship masculinities to be open to all men, not in spite but because of the diversity of social locations and experiences among us? We take up epistemological challenges for allyship masculinity including active ignorance, epistemic injustice, and situated knowledge, before turning to social, political, and ethical challenges, with particular attention to issues of accountability and male privilege put toward feminist ends within patriarchal systems.

**Keywords** Accountability • Allyship • Epistemic injustice • Feminist epistemology • Intersectionality • Masculinity • Privilege • Standpoint theory

In the previous chapter I argued that feminist allyship opens up conceptual space for a normative alternative to toxic masculinity not just consistent with but actively grounded in feminist values and projects. It does not appeal to some elusive essential difference between men and women, but in differentiating itself from feminist androgyny, it also shows how virtuous human qualities like compassion or courage exhibited by those who embody masculinity and also how those who do not can fit within a relational conception of allyship. My account builds on bell hooks' vision for feminist manhood, Linda Alcoff's work on anti-racist whiteness, and a socially situated analysis of allyship generally and of men's feminist allyship more specifically. In this chapter, I want to think more expansively about the challenges for feminist allyship masculinity in social context. Among other things, this might help us see the intersectional possibilities of allyship masculinity—what it looks like in practice for allyship masculinities to be accessible to differently positioned men, not despite but because of the considerable diversity of social locations and experiences among us.

## Deeply Nonideal Masculinity

Consider a contrast between allyship masculinity and the mythopoetic masculinity of Robert Bly's *Iron John* (1990), Bill Kauth's *Circle of Men* (1992), or Sam Keen's *Fire in the Belly* (1992). Like the ideal of androgyny, allyship and mythopoetic masculinities oppose gender roles and divisions as conventionally configured in modern society, but unlike feminist androgyny their opposition to traditional masculinity is taken as grounds for reformation rather than abolition. The "new heroic man" is full of wonder, humility, and empathy, Keen says; but he is not androgynous, not a blend of masculine and feminine characteristics. "In my own experiences, I can locate nothing that feels 'feminine' about holding my daughter in my arms," he writes. "Nor do I feel 'masculine' when I am chopping wood or riding my horse down a steep mountain trail" (1992, 213). These are just stereotypes, labels. "Once we have stripped away all the false mystification of gender, an authentic mystery of gender remains. Beneath the facade of socially constructed differences between men and women, there is a genuine mystery of biological and ontological differences" (1992, 217).

What's fascinating and confusing about Keen's simultaneous critique of gender stereotypes and celebration of authentic manhood echoes J.J. Bola's (2019, 118) characterization of masculinity as both a mask and one's true face to be revealed. Gender is real and binary, Keen says, just not in the way we were taught to perform it. "God did not make persons–chairpersons, mailpersons, or spokespersons–only men and women. Peel away the layers of social conditioning and there remains the prime fact of the duality of men and women" (1992, 218). This celebration of "the communion of opposites–in love and sex" (1992, 219) reflects a commitment to gender essentialism typical of mythopoetic masculinity (Clatterbaugh 1995, 49) that runs roughshod across the diverse range of human experiences. By contrast, to whatever extent participating in allyship masculinity involves building solidarity with other men, it is not to separate from what Keen calls a *world of WOMEN*—"larger-than-life shadowy female figures who inhabit our imaginations, inform our emotions, and indirectly give shape to many of our actions" (1992, 13)—in order to find an essentially masculine self. To whatever extent allyship masculinity directs us to look inward, it is not to uncover some primal, authentic manhood deep within. As Bob Pease (2000, 117) aptly puts it, "If we are talking about evolving non-patriarchal masculinities, they have to be as socially constructed as the patriarchal masculinities."

Allyship masculinity as I have tried to describe it is a decidedly nonideal thing. By this I do not mean that it is inadequate or second-rate, but that it would not have the substance that it does under ideal conditions. It is in the aftermath of injustice where allyship masculinity is made meaningful. (By *aftermath* I mean only that injustice has been done, not necessarily that it has since stopped.) Given our histories, institutions, and systems of oppression, what does feminist masculinity look like? It is admittedly not an easy question to answer, which is one reason I appreciate the epistemic humility that Tom Digby (2014, 149) and Jared Yates Sexton (2019, 252) bring to their respective critical analyses of toxic masculinity. But the contingency of allyship masculinity is a feature, not a bug. As with those who advocate an ideal of androgyny, we can hope and plan for a possible future where systemic, wide-sweeping gender justice has made normative masculinity an obsolete category. And yet this does not mean we should now act as if it is already obsolete. What allyship masculinities offer are critically reflective, substantively feminist ways men can be—not forever and always, but for the unjust meantime. "Our work should not aim to produce ideals capable of serving as permanent standards of assessments for all societies," Alison Jaggar (2019, 17–18) argues for philosophical investigations beyond the armchair; "instead like the results of scientific investigations, the ideals we produce should be taken as provisional, subject to change as our circumstances change." My own account of feminist allyship masculinities is offered in this spirit, where contingency and openness to change as the circumstances of justice change are constitutive elements rather than inadvertent or unwelcome areas of incompletion.

## Intersectionality Revisited

I have focused on men's distinctive relationships and potential contributions to feminist projects in an effort to show how these contributions can be valuable and constitutive of a meaningfully feminist masculinity. But this is not to say men should limit their contributions to emancipatory and reparative projects to only those things that are distinctive to their social positioning as men. For one thing, there are of course many actions large and small that men, women, and non-binary people can all do to contribute to gender justice; simply because these things are not as connected to our specific social locations does not necessarily make them less important. Further, as social identities are not exhausted nor fully constituted by gender alone, our allyship practices needn't be limited to those that are constitutive of masculinity, even an alternate to masculinity as traditionally configured. Following Alcoff, we might recognize anti-racist white histories and communities as themselves constituting an alternate whiteness available to those who do the work. For white men, the work of anti-racist allyship sometimes may also be the work of feminist allyship: these allyship practices are constitutive of both anti-racist whiteness and feminist masculinity. At other times the tasks of dismantling racism and patriarchy might be distinct (which is not to say in conflict) and even when the projects themselves converge, the work of anti-racist white allyship may be distinct from (again, not necessarily contrary to) the work of men's feminist allyship. Consider for example anti-racist allyship practices that call for similar contributions from white allies across gender, or feminist work to which men's gender identities and experiences make a difference even as other aspects of our social identities are less relevant to the specific task at hand. Consider contributions of Frederick Douglass, W.E.B. DuBois, and other feminist forefathers not only to androcentric racial justice but also to progressive gender activism (Guy-Sheftall 2006, 43; Byrd and Guy-Sheftall 2001). The point is not that our allyship practices must or even should always be clearly delineated and identifiable nor that we should always know which allyship practices are constitutive of what parts of our (or others') social identities. Taking intersectional allyship seriously does not simply mean recognizing our contributions to feminist projects as aligned with or as orthogonal to other liberatory and ameliorative collective responses to historical and existing systems of oppression. It also means that as men vary in our social locations, those distinctive contributions that we are well-positioned to make toward feminist and other projects sometimes also will vary.

Intersecting axes of oppression mean that men in the fullness of their social identities can be both beneficiaries and victims of gender injustices. Sexism, racism, and other forms of oppression cannot always be neatly disentangled without losing what is explanatorily significant about these oppressive structures and about how victims experience them. As Nico Juarez puts it, "People tend to think about intersectionality as adding up all their oppressions and their privileges to know where they are. In reality, when you add masculinity into Nativeness, they aren't simply adding a privilege to an oppressed category; you are radically changing both" (Plank 2019, 249). To say that men of color experience discrimination, injustice, and oppression only and always in virtue of being people of color and never in virtue of being men of color is to presume a narrowly additive conception of racism and sexism (Spelman 1988, 114; Mutua 2006, 22).

We can see these tensions in Tommy Curry's critique of mainstream feminist philosophy in his book *The Man-Not* (2017) and Olufemi Taiwo's (2018) critical defense of intersectional feminism in response (see also Pennyamon 2015; Oluwayomi 2020). Curry argues that scholars generally and intersectional feminist theorists specifically fail to do justice to Black men and boys and the material conditions of their lives; over and over again, he says, they marginalize, pathologize, and erase Black American male experience. Taiwo agrees that it is too simple to assert that Black males are disadvantaged by racism and advantaged by sexism: "the intersection of Blackness and maleness is poorly theorized by analogy to, say, whiteness and maleness" (2018, 7). But he is less convinced by Curry's opposition to intersectionality. In fact, "against the advice of the text itself, I read *The Man-Not* as a work of intersectional theory," he observes. "I suspect this conclusion will be equally unwelcome to the author and the overlapping sets of scholars that the book makes it its business to criticize" (2018, 8). As Taiwo sees it, Curry is not solely to blame for the tension and confusion here; intersectionality is even more complicated than many advocates and critics would seem to appreciate. "It will take difficult and complex empirical work to sort out what our generalizations should be regarding different intersectional categories of people," Taiwo argues, "whether Black males or any other" (2018, 9). The good news is that a more expansive and empirically grounded intersectional feminism can not only accommodate Curry's insights about the undertheorized and mischaracterized experiences of Black American men and boys, but actively center and build around them (see also Crenshaw 1991, 1258; Mutua 2012, 341).

Recognizing that men can be targets of intersectional gender oppression does not mean that all men experience gender-based oppression, nor does it deny that men taken collectively pervasively and systematically enjoy gender-based privileges and entitlements. What it does mean is that while some men's allyship masculinity may derive primarily from constructive grappling with our male privilege and ignorance, for others it is more complicated. This again is a benefit of recognizing feminist allyship masculinities pluralized and characterizing allyship in a way that emphasizes difference but does not assume that allies by definition can never also be targets of the oppressive systems to be dismantled.

## What Men Can Know

It is a fool's errand to look for something that all and only men know, as much it would be to seek something equally universal and ubiquitous across all women's knowledge. Fortunately, feminist epistemologies offer more nuanced accounts of the relation between gender and knowledge. What these varied philosophies have in common is a recognition that social locations make an epistemic difference, and that gender is a significant aspect of social location. Who we are and how we are positioned in the world affect the experiences we are likely to have, observations we are likely to make, and how we interpret those experiences and observations (Code 2006).

When it comes to knowledge and ignorance in a world shot-through with gender discrimination and oppression, there is not necessarily one main way this works. Many contributions to the recent literature on epistemic injustice identify various ways that people are wronged in their capacity as knowers generally, and specifically how identity stereotypes and social structures can underwrite gender-based epistemic wrongs (Fricker 2007; Dotson 2011; Pohlhaus 2012; McKinnon 2016). Recall the pointed critiques in Chap. 2 from Wollstonecraft (1792) and Macaulay (1790) on how gendered education deprives girls and women of training and understanding of traditionally male domains. Macaulay is especially perceptive about how boys and men are left ignorant of the skills and knowledge required in traditionally feminine domains because of their own highly gendered and incomplete education. More recently, feminist social epistemologists have built upon Charles Mills' (2007) account of white ignorance to show how gendered gaps in knowledge are not simply the passive result of attention paid elsewhere: sometimes ignorance is actively constructed, where the *not-knowing* is itself the point (Alcoff 2007). We might also recall John Stuart Mill's discussion of epistemic arrogance and other intellectual vices in boys and men in gender inequitable societies. Marginalization of female voices not only erodes their epistemic agency and deprives the world of their insights, but also overinflates the regard that boys and men have of their own intelligence (Rossi 1970, 218).

Feminist standpoint theorists advance this analysis further, showing how social and epistemic privileges are inversely related under patriarchy, heteronormativity, and other oppressive systems. It is not just that oppressive systems deprive marginalized people of valuable epistemic resources and devalue their perspectives (though standpoint theorists recognize these things too) but further that marginalization enables a *better* understanding of social reality within an oppressive system. This epistemic privilege is not automatic, Alison Wylie (2012) argues. Developing a standpoint is an achievement, the result of sustained critical reflection on gendered experiences rather than an essential or inherent female way of knowing (Toole 2021). As Sandra Harding explains, a feminist standpoint *begins* and is *grounded in* women's experiences, a starting point for critical inquiry in contrast to androcentric inquiries that treat men's lives as their presumptive basis (1992, 450; see also Harding 1990, 1991; Hirsch et al. 1995).

One lesson to take from this varied work is that men and boys are not exempt from the effects of the fraught relationship between gender and knowledge. Men are not only responsible for the harms of epistemic injustice but also negatively impacted by them: sometimes as victims of racial, ethnic, class, or other identity stereotypes, and even when not as victims, epistemically worse off due to credibility mismatches and unfilled gaps in understanding of significant social experiences. Men's intellectual virtues are stunted by gender inequity, and our ignorance of the fullness of the world and human social experience of it is actively constructed. And because men are not just men generically, because gender partially but does not on its own fully constitute our social locations, men's knowledge and ignorance is further affected by white supremacy, heteronormativity, and other oppressive systems. For some, our ignorance is constructed as a shield to protect our race, class, or other unearned privileges; some are marginalized and subjected to epistemic injustices by white supremacy and heteronormativity; and some have intersecting, overlapping, and conflicting experiences as both beneficiaries and victims of oppressive social systems in their complicated, confusing, sometimes contradictory manifestations.

Consider the situation of men who are members of a community in which sexual harassment and discrimination are endemic problems, yet who do not believe that they have seen these things themselves. Other men in this community do recognize that they have witnessed sexual harassment and discrimination, of course; some have been targets themselves. On first analysis, these men might treat their absence of personal observation as counterevidence against the pervasiveness of sexism in their community, and might say as much in community forums. In this case, the norms of allyship masculinity ask such men to consider how their gendered social positions as men may be relevant to their not-witnessing sexism that exists in their community. "Is my not-witnessing better understood as counterevidence or as a sort of gendered ignorance?" one should ask. Allyship masculinity also means considering the significance of one's testimony of not-witnessing sexism in its social-epistemic context, namely, in response to others' testimonies of firsthand experiences of sexual harassment and discrimination. "What is the *point* of my not-witnessing testimony?" we should ask ourselves. "Is it making a constructive contribution to our collective understanding, or is it instead obscuring the issue?" Different men will answer these questions differently, given the specific details of their lives and their specific situations.

To be sure, testimonial injustice, testimonial smothering, and other forms of epistemic violence are not unique to men nor are they limited to gender oppression. My claim here is not that virtuous listening is uniquely constitutive of allyship masculinity. To the extent that existing patriarchal systems serve to configure our experiences differently along gender lines, allyship masculinity asks men to consider how our distinctively gendered experiences make a difference, for better or worse, and take these considerations into account in our beliefs and actions.

Part of allyship masculinity, then, is being mindful of how one's particular social position as a man within a patriarchal society affects one's knowledge and ignorance, and how these epistemic effects may be different for one's allies including differently positioned men, women, and non-binary people. Here someone might rightly note that women and non-binary people should also be mindful of how their own areas of knowledge and ignorance are affected by their social positions under patriarchy. This is indeed true. How then is an epistemic mindfulness distinctly constitutive of not just feminist identity generally but feminist masculinity specifically? There is theoretical and practical overlap between men's and others' feminist allyship, to be sure. Taking a cue from the ideal of androgyny, we might imagine a future in which people should be mindful of how their social locations might affect their knowledge and ignorance even though gender identity no longer factors into that awareness. In the unjust meantime, however, the fact that one is a man rather than a woman or non-binary person is explanatorily significant. It makes an epistemic difference, even as the difference it makes is not the same for all men.

Given the imperative from feminist standpoint theory to start research from marginalized lives, how if at all can men contribute to knowledge-making from social locations where we ourselves do not live? Call this the *methodological-epistemological challenge* for men's feminist allyship. Some men might despair (or alternately delight) in the apparent implication that we are excluded (or excused) from participating in research projects from marginalized lives. But this implication need not follow: the methodological-epistemological challenge is notable but not insurmountable. For one thing, the diversity among men means that many of us are already part of historically marginalized communities whose needs, values, and ways of life have been historically excluded, objectified, and misrepresented by Western science. The feminist call to start research in women's lives aligns and overlaps with postcolonial calls to start research in the lives of Indigenous peoples and people of color worldwide (Harding 2008). Furthermore, for all the emphasis put upon the inverse relationship between social and epistemic privilege, standpoint theory is neither separatist nor relativist in its aims or methods. In contrast to those at the top, Harding explains, "the activities of those at the bottom of such social hierarchies can provide starting points for thought–for *everyone's* research and scholarship–from which humans' relations with each other and the natural world can become visible" (1992, 442–443). After all, standpoint methodology is not for individual women to ground their thought exclusively in their own specific social locations, nor for women collectively to agree on a single ideal woman's life from which to begin. The idea is that everyone involved (including but not just men) will contribute to research that at least sometimes starts from lives that are different from our own. This is not necessarily a cause for skeptical concern, as Uma Narayan explains. "Our commitment to the contextual nature of knowledge does not require us to claim that those who do not inhabit these contexts can never have any knowledge of them" (2003, 314). Harding herself has long made it clear that men are neither excluded nor excused from the collective enterprise:

> Men's thought, too, will begin first from women's lives in all the ways that feminist theory, with its rich and contradictory tendencies, has helped us all—women as well as men—to understand how to do. It will start there in

order to gain the maximally objective theoretical frameworks within which men can begin to describe and explain *their own and women's lives* in less partial and distorted ways. (1992, 457)

Following Harding and Narayan, men can take up the methodological-epistemological challenge of knowing across gender difference. We do not have to be driven to do so because of our anxieties, tempting as that might be, but because doing so enables more accurate knowledge of human lives including our own. The work of knowing across difference is neither downplayed nor dismissed, but rather embraced as a collective project with considerable social-epistemic potential.

Still the preceding discussion should not obscure the fact that starting thought in women's lives can be a challenge for men raised to take androcentrism for granted. Reckoning with, meeting, and even failing at this challenge are themselves constitutive practices of feminist allyship masculinity. Overcoming bystander paralysis and contributing to collective thought that begins from women's lives is a start, but this alone is not enough. Having goodwill toward one's feminist allies is also a good thing, but this alone is not enough either. "It is a commonplace that even sympathetic men will often fail to perceive subtle instances of sexist behavior or discourse," Narayan reminds us. "Sympathetic individuals who are not members of oppressed groups should keep in mind the possibility of this sort of failure regarding their understanding of issues relating to an oppression they do not share" (2003, 314).

Narayan's warning need not spur a retreat to skepticism or relativism, but rather a reiteration of the need for accountability in allyship across difference. In interviews with dozens of men active in gender violence prevention, Messner et al. (2015, 162) notice a difference of opinions on the politics of accountability. Where men like Paul Kivel (1992) see a close connection between allyship and accountability to women, other men do not seem to see it that way. Of anti-violence groups working exclusively with men, John Erickson reasons, "it's just all men, I don't think they'd have to be held accountable to anyone" (Messner et al. 2015, 167). "Am I accountable to women, like no? Yes? It's just an odd question," says Stephen Philp:

> I feel like I'm pretty confident that I know what a pro-gender-equality behavior is, you know, like I've been doing this long enough at this point and I'm firmly established enough in my feminist identity that I feel like I'm

pretty capable on my own at figuring out what to do, and because of a lot of my involvement, even at this point, involves women, I don't feel like I need to explicitly get their approval. (Messner et al. 2015, 167)

Gilbert Salazar, also experienced in anti-violence work with men, voices some similar reservations about the need for accountability:

> Being accountable to women, I personally don't sort of—doesn't strike me as something that seems very positive. Why should I be accountable to someone, anyone, not just women? I mean that's really where my independence really wants to come in and I just wanna fight and be like, 'Why can't we be accountable to each other?' (Messner et al. 2015, 167)

I am with Kivel rather than Erickson, Philp, or Salazar on this. But I do wonder if the disagreement here might turn on some questionable assumptions about what accountability involves as much as anything else. Being accountable to our allies means being open to, actively inviting, and learning from their critical feedback (see Goldrick-Jones 2002; Atherton-Zeman 2011; Pease 2017; Bourke 2020). It means recognizing allies as epistemic collaborators and knowers in their own right, not merely sources of information or useful instruments for furthering one's own knowledge (Fricker 2007, 6; Dotson 2008, 58; Berenstain 2016, 570). But it does not demand epistemic deference to one's allies nor treating them as if they are infallible, which Narayan reminds us "may reduce itself to another subtle form of condescension" (2003, 315; see also Taiwo 2020). Our different social locations do make a difference to relations of accountability, but it need not be a one-way street. Salazar is right to suggest that maybe we all need to be accountable to each other; where he goes wrong is in raising this as counting against men's accountability to women rather than advocating it as a more complicated and ultimately more constructive web of accountability among feminist allies.

## PUTTING PRIVILEGE TO WORK

There is work toward gender equity and undoing oppression to which allies across gender identities can contribute in similar ways, just as there are truths about the world which we can recognize in similar ways. Yet one recurring recommendation among those who write about and lead programs on allyship is that men should identify and take advantage of opportunities to put their privilege to work for justice.

When it comes to contributing to collective projects toward dismantling gender oppression, men are better situated to make some contributions than others, and sometimes better positioned than women are to make particular sorts of contributions. There are, as James Sterba notes, "many contexts in which men are good for feminism, that is, many contexts in which men can make useful contributions to the cause of feminism" (1998, 298). Sterba urges feminist men to argue for gender equality in spaces in which women are underrepresented and to actively use their male privilege to advocate for gender equality in conversations with those who extend greater credibility to men than women. Jonathan Ravarino (2013, 160) likewise argues that, "as men, we have unique access to other men. This same-sex dynamic means that men can be effective social justice allies in addressing sensitive topics" (see also Drury and Kaiser 2014, 643; Smith and Johnson 2020, 10). In addition to issues of credibility, men sometimes might be more willing and able to appraise their male privilege and complicity in patriarchal systems honestly alongside other, similarly implicated men. This is not to say men working with men or other such distinctively gendered contributions to dismantling oppression are more important than other contributions—far from it. But we can see how men's committed, accountable, and reflective contributions to feminist work can themselves give meaning to a distinctively feminist sort of masculinity.

I raised concerns for Kimmel's model of new masculinity in *Manhood in America* (1996) and *Guyland* (2008). But elsewhere Kimmel sees a distinctive role for men in a sort of Gentlemen's Auxiliary of Feminism: "an honorable position, one that acknowledges that this is a revolution of which we are part, but not the central part, not its most significant part," he explains. "It will be the task of a Gentleman's Auxiliary to make feminism comprehensible to men, not as a loss of power…but as a challenge to that false sense of entitlement to that power in the first place" (Kimmel 1998, 67). *Guyland* includes examples of how men can make distinct contributions to undoing gender oppression. Kimmel shares the story of a fraternity member reconsidering his complicity in the "walk of shame," as fraternity brothers gathered to heckle sorority sisters heading home on weekend mornings after hooking up. Inspired by Kimmel's recent visit, this man found like-minded fraternity members opposed to the heckling. After discussion among themselves, they took their opposition to their fraternity, made their case, and effected small but meaningful local change (2008, 281). Kimmel sees in this man's efforts a genuine attempt to get beyond the limits of his experiences and to stand against injustice as others experience it. Notice that this fraternity member did not oppose injustice in a generic way, but from his specific social situation within a highly gendered cultural institution. His experience of the walk of shame differed from the women who endured it, and his position in the fraternity allowed him an avenue for change that was unavailable to these women and other outsiders.

Opportunities and obligations to put gender privilege to work are not limited to the straight, white, cisgender young men of Guyland. In his own writings (McBee 2014, 2018) and in conversation with Liz Plank (2019), Thomas Page McBee describes the "shocking turn" of male privilege after coming out as trans: "when I spoke, people didn't just listen, they leaned in," McBee says. "It was as if whatever I said, however banal, was surely worth that strain of a neck, or the hurried quieting of all other thoughts." This unearned clout was a blessing and curse: "more than once, I would catch myself midramble and wonder, 'Am I mansplaining?'" (2018). "He suddenly was seen as part of a group he didn't always wholeheartedly endorse," Plank (2019, 21–22) tells us. "Armed with this newly found male privilege, Thomas suddenly felt a responsibility to effect change." Among other things, this meant using his voice to highlight the often marginalized yet essential labor and unacknowledged accomplishments of his female co-workers. More generally, McBee (2018) says, "I got better at doing the things that, as a man, I had been recently socialized not to do: asking for help, giving credit for it and admitting that I didn't have all the answers."

In the concluding chapter of *How to Raise a Feminist Son*, Sonora Jha shares a powerful story in which her teenage son used his male privilege to advocate for her—not in a professional setting, but in a difficult conversation with Jha's mother while traveling together in India. Jha's mother adores her grandson, doting on him, calling him "a god" more than once. So when she completely denies her daughter's painful experience and her testimony of sexual assault growing up in India (which Jha left as an adult, and to which her mother is urging her to return), the son comes to his mother's aid. He uses his male privilege not only to coax his grandmother to take seriously a truth that she stubbornly denies, but more than this, to move her to empathize with her daughter as he himself does. "Maybe you can believe her *this time*?" he asks. "You will know you have raised a feminist son," Jha (2021, 230) writes proudly, "when he uses the voice he has been given–some might even say the voice of a god—to be the best kind of ally."

The imperative to put one's male privilege to work toward feminist ends is an important part of what makes feminist allyship a meaningfully normative alternative to toxic masculinity, and yet actually putting this norm into practice may not be as easy or straightforward as it seems. "The act of using your privilege to dismantle the very system that confers your privilege can feel unnatural," Smith and Johnson (2020, 36) acknowledge. The tensions involved in putting male privilege to work to feminist ends are not only psychological but also social, political, and economic. Consider *the pedestal effect*, where men working in violence prevention and similar fields "are frequently given more attention and respect, basically for saying the same things that women have been saying for years" (Messner et al. 2015, 138; also Atherton-Zeman 2011; Peretz 2020). The pedestal effect is not experienced uniformly by all men who do such work. It is racialized as well as gendered, such that men of color often receive more scrutiny and suspicion than their white counterparts or women in these fields (Messner et al. 2015, 143).

A related issue is what Christine Williams calls *the glass escalator*, wherein men who enter predominantly female professions in contrast to women who enter predominantly male professions "generally encounter structural advantages in these occupations which tend to enhance their careers" (1992, 253). Williams finds that while straight, white, middle-class men in elementary education, nursing, and social work may well face discrimination from those outside the field, this is not generally so for hiring, promotion, and other such evaluations that are made from within. "Men take their gender privilege with them when they enter predominantly female occupations" (1992, 264). (For intersectional analyses of the glass escalator phenomenon, see Wingfield 2009; Williams 2013.)

On the one hand we might see the pedestal and glass escalator effects as further opportunity for men to put their privileges to good ends, in this case, using that unearned celebration to draw more attention to important ideas and projects. But the privileges involved here are not limited to the messages conveyed or work done—it is not the messages nor the work that are put on a pedestal, after all. At stake are not only which messages are successfully conveyed in contexts where they had received no hearing, or even who gets intellectual credit and who continues to be ignored, but also whose positions receive funding, book contracts signed, lucrative consultations secured with academic, military, governmental, and corporate partners, and so on (Messner et al. 2015, 149).

Related to the pedestal effect and glass escalator for men doing what has traditionally been cast as women's work is what we might call *the master's tools problem*. Underlying the imperative to put male privilege to work toward feminist ends is the idea that such privileges, though unearned and unfair, are nevertheless useful—and not just useful to reinforce existing systems of oppression. Yet if we heed Audre Lorde's (1984) warning that the master's tools will never dismantle the master's house, *can* unearned gender privilege be used to dismantle systems of gender injustice? Try as we might, won't these tools of injustice inevitably reproduce what they were made for? Consider for example *embodied athletic masculinity*, which Messner, Greenberg, and Peretz call "the adjustable power drill in the master's toolkit" for anti-violence work with boys and men. Embodied athletic masculinity opens doors, lends credibility, and captures attention. "Is it possible to use this tool to dismantle the privileges of masculinity?" they ask (2015, 148). "Or might we expect that the use of the master's tools will, at best, poke some holes in or file off some of the jagged edges of masculinity, while reinforcing the privileges of those who embody it?"

One option is to deny the premise and insist that the master's tools can be put to new purposes. This seems to be Jackson Katz's response:

> I know this gets complicated and I appreciate that, and I've *always* been self-reflexively thinking about, 'OK, I'm using hegemonic masculinity to deconstruct hegemonic masculinity,' which is what I am doing. I always took that quote from Audre Lorde, 'You can't use the master's tools to take apart the master's house,' and the first time I heard it I thought, "This is completely wrong, this is completely wrong.' It's like, Audre Lorde is a writer, *she's* using the master's tools—writing is the most dominant tool of the hegemonic culture—to deconstruct the master's house. So it's internally contradictory in addition to being problematic as a political strategy. (As quoted in Messner et al. 2015, 148–149)

For their part, Messner and coauthors agree that Katz has indeed used the master's tools (including his own athletic masculinity) to gain access to the master's house, specifically to male-dominated spaces like football locker rooms, frat houses, and military. This is no small feat: as Alison Bailey suggests, "Although the master's tools may not be able to successfully dismantle the master's house, they may be just the tools we need to gain access to its contents" (1999, 102). Once inside, do bystander trainings in the master's house have the power to tear it down from within?

I cannot pretend to offer a comprehensive solution to the master's tools problem, but it bears repeating that navigating this challenge is itself a constitutive part of feminist allyship masculinity. Grappling with, succeeding, even failing to put one's male privilege to work in service of gender justice without thereby reinforcing existing configurations of gender oppression is itself a crucial norm of feminist masculinity, of what feminist men as feminists and as men should do. Others in social justice movements experience their own versions of the master's tools problem too: Lorde, after all, put the challenge directly to an audience of white women ostensibly committed to working with women of color. And different men must grapple with this challenge in different ways, since the privileges that they might put toward feminist projects will vary across differently positioned men. Still I find it meaningful to see this challenge as itself part of the work of allyship masculinity when it involves distinctly male privileges toward feminist ends from within patriarchal cultures and institutions.

Like Alcoff's account of anti-racist white identity, histories, and communities, one thing that drives my approach to allyship masculinity is the recognition that unearned social privileges in an unjust social world are not always something one can decline. Such privileges will be extended anyway, with or without the recipient's approval. So as we grapple with the master's tools problem, it may be useful to distinguish between *forced* and *avoidable* privileges: that is, between privileges that are inescapable and those that may or may not be operative depending on the circumstances, including what one does and how one does it. This is somewhat like William James' (1896, 329) distinction between forced and avoidable beliefs, where the former can't be avoided but must be held in one way or another. Forced privileges for many (which is not to say all) men in patriarchal societies include having one's resume viewed favorably compared to an equally qualified woman's resume, not having one's words misconstrued or mischaracterized based on dismissive gender stereotypes, and having standard consumer goods designed to fit one's needs, among other things. Avoidable privileges might include the power to interrupt women without consequence, raising or projecting one's voice to garner more attention and credibility, owning property, holding political office, etc. This is not to say that forced privileges are better or worse than avoidable ones, nor that avoidable privileges should always be avoided because they can. Indeed, sometimes they should be exercised toward feminist ends.

It might also be useful to distinguish between *zero-sum* and *nonzero-sum* privileges, those that benefit the recipient at others' expense and those that benefit the recipient but without necessarily harming others (Von Neumann and Morgenstern 2007, 238; Mutua 2006, 35; McKinnon and Sennet 2017, 3). We can identify many zero-sum privileges that men in patriarchal societies tend to enjoy at others' expense, including the aforementioned gender-biased evaluation of comparable resumes, holding political offices barred to women, institutional privileges in sexual harassment and assault cases, or even something as mundane as the default thermostat settings in an office environment. Other privileges that men enjoy benefit them and are indeed gendered in a patriarchal society but also would be beneficial in a gender-equitable world (McIntosh 1988). Nonzero-sum privileges may include having medicines and goods made to fit one's needs, having the freedom to walk at night without fear of sexual assault, or having one's words successfully and accurately communicated as intended.

Last but not least, we might distinguish between applications of male privilege that *destabilize* unjust distributions of gender privilege and systems of oppression generally and those that tend to *reinforce* them. This last distinction may be especially useful to defend Lorde from Katz's charge of internal contradiction. Which are the tools that will never dismantle the master's house: merely something the master happens to use toward his oppressive ends? Something made to be used for these ends? Or something that cannot or probably cannot be used successfully without furthering or reproducing these oppressive ends? I submit that the last of these is the temptation that Lorde illuminates and the temptation we must avoid. When she urges white feminists not to fall into the trap of building solidarity around women's similarities and ignoring their differences, what makes this a master's tool in the third sense is that doing so will inevitably reproduce the presumptive prioritization of the experiences of the most dominant members of the group, just as it does when men insist that social justice movements must transcend what "divides" us, that we should not get distracted by so-called women's issues or other "special interests." Writing meanwhile is a tool in the first sense. Katz is correct, of course, that the written word is widely used by the hegemonic culture—but that does not mean writing cannot also be put to radically different ends, as centuries of human history can attest.

The call to put our privileges to work seems most compelling when the privileges in question are avoidable, nonzero-sum, and destabilizing, cases in which we conceivably could refuse to take advantage of some privilege and yet as feminist allies we have good reason not to. Forced privilege cannot be avoided (though we may sometimes fool ourselves otherwise) but can be directed toward destabilizing or reinforcing ends, as for example when a man uses the fact that his words will most likely be accurately communicated to a certain audience to argue for the credibility of women or non-binary speakers whom this audience has misjudged, or instead uses that misjudgment to sell one's oppositional position. Most troubling is when men put their privileges to work in ways are avoidable, zero-sum, and reinforce a patriarchal status quo.

What should we say, then, about embodied athletic masculinity in gender violence prevention and Katz's self-described "use of hegemonic masculinity to deconstruct hegemonic masculinity"? Some elements of embodied athletic masculinity like an ex-linebacker's height and general build will be present no matter what one does or refrains from doing. Meanwhile many other elements can be evoked selectively and situationally: not just height and build but how we hold ourselves, myriad choices made in both verbal and nonverbal communication, interactions with and reactions to others, the stories we tell and how we choose to tell them. Men capable of embodying athletic masculinity so understood might not do so deliberately, but at least some of these elements are optional privileges that may or may not be used, and may or may not be used to various ends.

Part of what is interesting about embodied athletic masculinity is its uneasy relationship with toxic gender configurations. If hegemonic masculinity can be used to deconstruct itself, as Katz says, the project will be necessarily limited, one part of hegemonic masculinity used to destabilize another: for example, when core values and rhetoric drawn from men's sports, fraternities, or the military are celebrated and reified in service of the specific goal of encouraging men as men to prevent violence against women. The larger point of dispute between those who use and those who criticize embodied athletic masculinity in men's active bystander trainings seems to concern *how much* of hegemonic masculinity needs to be dismantled. Do existing cultures and institutions such as collegiate and professional football, fraternities, and the military only need to be reformed, or does taking gender-based violence and gender-based systems of oppression generally seriously mean these paradigmatically toxic masculine cultures and institutions must be utterly dismantled? For those who believe the latter, the call to use hegemonic masculinity against itself is a master's tools problem: tempting because its hegemony makes this seem like the only option, but ultimately reinforcing rather than destabilizing the oppressive structures that feminists are allied against.

## Relational Allyship and Accountability

Being able to distinguish between different kinds of male privilege may give us some guidance in navigating the master's tools problem for feminist allyship. But part of this problem is that it is not always easy to know whether a particular privilege we enjoy is forced or avoidable, nor whether a particular privilege that we rely upon in our contributions to gender justice in the unjust meantime is coming at others' expense. This is one more reason to underscore the relational aspect of feminist allyship masculinity, where the difference-in-common characteristic of ally relationships expands our collective resources for responding to the master's tools challenge.

The last thing a man should do is to rely entirely on his own uncorroborated and unchallenged independent judgment about when and how to put his privilege to work toward collective feminist ends. Even in the best of times, the failure to expose our beliefs and judgments to external critique undermines their epistemic strength, and for men educated and enculturated in patriarchal societies our beliefs and judgments are epistemically weakened further still by having been systematically shielded from women's criticisms and contrary arguments. The lessons from the previous section on epistemic injustice, ignorance, and accountability carry this warning further still: that what men don't know may itself be a form of active ignorance constructed in our or others' interests. These countervailing epistemic considerations should give men pause in trusting our unchallenged and uncorroborated senses of success in putting our privileges to work toward feminist ends without thereby reinforcing unjust social configurations. For that matter, we should also reflect critically on the decision *not* to put our male privileges to work toward feminist ends for fear of perpetrating further wrongdoing in the process.

The social-epistemic resource of trustworthy allyship across difference undercuts paralyzing conclusions about men's feminist contributions that a strictly individualistic analysis otherwise would invite. As Kivel (1992), Atherton-Zeman (2011), and others argue, standing in relationships of accountability can be enriching rather than demeaning for men as feminist allies—contrary to Salazar's worries, a positive thing indeed. Without accountability to other men, women, and non-binary people across social locations, men individually and collectively are all more epistemically impoverished, isolated within our partial perspectives, and so less capable of usefully contributing to dismantling systems of oppression.

Along with the epistemic benefits of differently positioned feminist allies sharing insights and perspectives comes the risk that ally relationships are vulnerable to gendered epistemic injustices. One relevant injustice is what Nora Berenstain (2016) calls *epistemic exploitation*, where socially marginalized and oppressed people are compelled to do the often undervalued and uncompensated epistemic labor needed to educate socially privileged people about the nature of their oppression. Does the relational approach to feminist allyship that I have advocated here presume that women and non-binary people should shoulder the heavy cognitive and practical burdens of educating men? Many men certainly seem to presume as much, that our interlocutors are compelled to answer our questions upon demand or take responsibility for our persisting ignorance (Berenstain 2016, 575; see also Lorde 1984; Jones 2004; Applebaum 2020). "Let me tell you what it feels like to stand in front of a white man and explain privilege to him." writes Manissa McCleave Maharawal (2011). "Every single time it is hard. Every single time I get angry that I have to do this, that this is my job, and that it shouldn't be my job."

As a normative nonideal model for men in the unjust meantime, feminist allyship masculinity must affirm that it should not be oppressed people's job to teach men about gender oppression and privilege. Whose job should it be? Taking responsibility for our own iterative education is among the norms of men's feminist allyship. Rather than excusing epistemic exploitation as a necessary burden that men's allies must bear in coalitional relationships, we recognize the labor of avoiding, anticipating, and ameliorating our own and others' gendered epistemic injustices as constitutive of allyship masculinity, as part of what men can and should distinctively contribute to feminist work. What this does not mean is that individual men should keep our own uncorroborated, unchallenged counsel, nor that accountability to our allies should become a hypothetical exercise. This need not be either solipsistic or exploitative. For one thing there are men, women, and non-binary people for whom teaching about gender and intersecting systems of oppression *is* our job, and spaces in which asking questions that may have been answered many times before is a suitable part of the process. Furthermore, whether we are inside or outside a classroom context, it is one thing to listen to you and another to compel you to speak, repeatedly and on demand. The truth is that nonbinary people, women, and men occupying social locations different than our own already are expressing themselves, already offer their constructive criticism, and have done so for a long time now. Their testimonies are available to be heard, even if we have not been listening or have not understood what is being said.

Finally, when feminist allyship is understood relationally, accountability to our allies becomes a dynamic activity. We acknowledge each other, listen to each other, stand up for each other, and along the way build trust. We make mistakes, yes, but we can also learn from our mistakes (or not) and in so doing give budding and potential allies further reason to invest (or shield) themselves in collaborating across difference. By our successes and failures in practicing feminist allyship from our positions as men within patriarchal systems, we show ourselves to be more or less trustworthy for differently positioned others. Realizing early opportunities for accountability lays a foundation for later, more specific and personal opportunities to learn from, engage with, and be accountable to our allies; missing these early opportunities makes deeper long-term relations of accountability that is much harder to build. Better understanding and being better understood are iterative processes. Like men's contributions to feminist politics and emancipatory projects more generally, they may not be quick or easy, but neither are they impossible or unprecedented. There is work we can do, relationships we can foster, and histories of feminist allyship by those who came before us in which we can find guidance and inspiration.

## References

Alcoff, Linda. 2007. Epistemologies of Ignorance: Three Types. In *Race and Epistemologies of Ignorance*, ed. Shannon Sullivan and Nancy Tuana, 39–58. Albany: SUNY Press.

Applebaum, Barbara. 2020. Racial Battle Fatigue, Epistemic Exploitation, and Willful Ignorance. *Philosophy of Education* 76 (4): 60–77.

Atherton-Zeman, Ben. 2011. We Can Do Better: 'Power and Control' and 'Accountability' Wheels for Male Aspiring Allies. *The Voice: The Journal of the Battered Women's Movement*: 32–33.

Bailey, Alison. 1999. Despising an Identity They Taught Me to Claim. In *Whiteness: Feminist Philosophical Narratives*, ed. Chris Cuomo and Kim Q. Hall, 85–107. Lanham: Rowman & Littlefield.
Berenstain, Nora. 2016. Epistemic Exploitation. *Ergo* 33 (2): 569–590.
Bly, Robert. 1990. *Iron John: A Book about Men*. Boston: Addison-Wesley.
Bola, J.J. 2019. *Mask Off: Masculinity Redefined*. London: Pluto Press.
Bourke, Brian. 2020. Leaving Behind the Rhetoric of Allyship. *Whiteness and Education* 5 (2): 179–194.
Byrd, Rudolph P., and Beverly Guy-Sheftall, eds. 2001. *Traps: African American Men on Gender and Sexuality*. Bloomington: Indiana University Press.
Clatterbaugh, Ken. 1995. Mythopoetic Foundations and New Age Patriarchy. In *The Politics of Manhood*, ed. Michael Kimmel, 44–63. Philadelphia: Temple University Press.
Code, Lorraine. 2006. *Ecological Thinking: The Politics of Epistemic Location*. Oxford: Oxford University Press.
Crenshaw, Kimberle. 1991. Mapping the Margins: Intersectionality, Identity Politics, and Violence against Women of Color. *Stanford Law Review* 43: 1241.
Curry, Tommy. 2017. *The Man-Not: Race, Class, Genre, and the Dilemmas of Black Manhood*. Philadelphia: Temple University Press.
Digby, Tom. 2014. *Love and War: How Militarism Shapes Sexuality and Romance*. New York: Columbia University Press.
Dotson, Kristie. 2008. In Search of Tanzania: Are Effective Epistemic Practices Sufficient for Just Epistemic Practices? *Southern Journal of Philosophy* 46: 52–64.
———. 2011. Tracking Epistemic Violence, Tracking Practices of Silencing. *Hypatia* 26 (2): 236–257.
Drury, Benjamin J., and Cheryl R. Kaiser. 2014. Allies against Sexism: The Role of Men in Confronting Sexism. *Journal of Social Issues* 70 (4): 637–652.
Fricker, Miranda. 2007. *Epistemic Injustice: Power and the Ethics of Knowing*. Oxford: Oxford University Press.
Goldrick-Jones, Amanda. 2002. *Men Who Believe in Feminism*. Westport: Praeger.
Guy-Sheftall, Beverly. 2006. Remembering Our Feminist Forefathers. In *Progressive Black Masculinities*, ed. Athena D. Mutua, 43–54. New York: Routledge.
Harding, Sandra. 1990. Starting Thought from Women's Lives: Eight Resources for Maximizing Objectivity. *Journal of Social Philosophy* 21 (2–3): 140–149.
———. 1991. *Whose Science? Whose Knowledge? Thinking from Women's Lives*. Ithaca: Cornell University Press.
———. 1992. Rethinking Standpoint Epistemology. *The Centennial Review* 36 (3): 437–470.
———. 2008. *Sciences from Below: Feminism, Postcolonialities, and Modernities*. Durham: Duke University Press.

Hirsch, Elizabeth, Gary Olsen, and Sandra Harding. 1995. Starting from Marginalized Lives: A Conversation with Sandra Harding. *JAC*: 193–225.
Jaggar, Alison. 2019. Thinking about Justice in the Unjust Meantime. *Feminist Philosophy Quarterly* 5 (2).
James, William. 1896. The Will to Believe. *The New World* 5: 327–347.
Jha, Sonora. 2021. *How to Raise a Feminist Son*. Seattle: Sasquatch.
Jones, Alison. 2004. Talking Cure: The Desire for Dialogue. *Counterpoints* 240: 57–67.
Katz, Jackson. (2006) 2019. *The Macho Paradox: Why Some Men Hurt Women and How All Men Can Help*. Naperville: Sourcebooks.
Kauth, Bill. 1992. *A Circle of Men*. New York: St. Martin's Press.
Keen, Sam. 1992. *Fire in the Belly: On Being a Man*. New York: Bantam Books.
Kimmel, Michael. 1996. *Manhood in America*. New York: The Free Press.
———. 1998. Who's Afraid of Men Doing Feminism? In *Men Doing Feminism*, ed. Tom Digby, 57–68. New York: Routledge.
———. 2008. *Guyland*. New York: HarperCollins.
Kivel, Paul. 1992. *Men's Work: How to Stop the Violence That Tears Our Lives Apart*. Center City: Hazelden Publishing.
Lorde, Audre. (1984) 2007. *Sister Outsider: Essays and Speeches*. Berkeley: Crossing Press.
Macaulay, Catharine. (1790) 2014. *Letters on Education*. Cambridge: Cambridge University Press.
Maharawal, Manissa McCleave. 2011. So Real It Hurts. *Occupied Wall Street Journal*. http://leftturn.org/so-real-it-hurts-notes-occupy-wall-street/.
McBee, Thomas Page. 2014. *Man Alive: A True Story of Violence, Forgiveness, and Becoming a Man*. San Francisco: City Lights Books.
———. 2018. My Voice Got Deeper, Suddenly People Listened. *New York Times*, August 9.
McIntosh, Peggy. 1988. White Privilege and Male Privilege. Center for Research on Women, Wellesley College.
McKinnon, Rachel. 2016. Epistemic Injustice. *Philosophy Compass* 11 (8): 437–446.
McKinnon, Rachel, and Adam Sennet. 2017. Survey Article: On the Nature of the Political Concept of Privilege. *Journal of Political Philosophy* 25 (4): 487–507.
Messner, Michael, Max Greenberg, and Tal Peretz. 2015. *Some Men: Feminist Allies and the Movement to End Violence against Women*. Oxford University Press.
Mills, Charles. 2007. White Ignorance. In *Race and Epistemologies of Ignorance*, ed. Shannon Sullivan and Nancy Tuana, 11–38. Albany: SUNY Press.
Mutua, Athena D. 2006. Theorizing Progressive Black Masculinities. In *Progressive Black Masculinities*, ed. D. Athena, 3–42. Mutua. New York: Routledge.
———. 2012. Multidimensionality is to Masculinities What Intersectionality is to Feminism. *Nevada Law Journal* 13: 341–367.

Narayan, Uma. 2003. The Project of Feminist Epistemology: Perspectives from a Non-Western Feminist. In *Feminist Theory Reader*, ed. Carole McCann and Seung-Kyung Kim, 308–317. New York: Routledge.
Oluwayomi, Adebayo. 2020. The Man-Not and the Inapplicability of Intersectionality to the Dilemmas of Black Manhood. *The Journal of Men's Studies* 28 (2): 183–205.
Pease, Bob. 2000. *Recreating Men: Postmodern Masculinity Politics*. Los Angeles: Sage.
———. 2017. *Men as Allies in Preventing Violence Against Women: Principles and Practices for Promoting Accountability*. Sydney: White Ribbon Australia.
Pennyamon, LaKeyma. 2015. Inversion and Invisibility: Black Women, Black Masculinity, and Anti-Blackness. *LIES Journal*, August.
Peretz, Tal. 2020. Seeing the Invisible Knapsack: Feminist Men's Strategic Responses to the Continuation of Male Privilege in Feminist Spaces. *Men and Masculinities* 23 (3–4): 447–475.
Plank, Liz. 2019. *For the Love of Men: A New Vision for Mindful Masculinity*. New York: St. Martin's Press.
Pohlhaus, Gaile. 2012. Relational Knowing and Epistemic Injustice: Toward a Theory of Willful Hermeneutical Injustice. *Hypatia* 27 (4): 715–735.
Ravarino, Jonathan. 2013. Being a Social Justice Ally. In *Men Speak Out*, ed. Shiva Tarrant, 174–181. New York: Routledge.
Rossi, Alice. ed. 1970. *Essays on Sex Equality*. Chicago: University of Chicago Press.
Sexton, Jared Yates. 2019. *The Man They Wanted Me to Be*. Berkeley: Counterpoint.
Smith, David G., and W. Brad Johnson. 2020. *Good Guys: How Men Can Be Better Allies for Women in the Workplace*. Boston, MA: Harvard Business Review Press.
Spelman, Elizabeth. 1988. *Inessential Woman: Problems of Exclusion in Feminist Thought*. Boston: Beacon Press.
Sterba, James. 1998. Is Feminism Good for Men and Are Men Good for Feminism? In *Men Doing Feminism*, ed. Tom Digby, 291–304. New York: Routledge.
Taiwo, Olufemi. 2018. *The Man Not* and the Dilemmas of Intersectionality. *APA Newsletter on Philosophy and the Black Experience* 17 (2): 6–10.
———. 2020. Being-in-the-Room Privilege: Elite Capture and Epistemic Deference. *The Philosopher* 108 (4): 61–70.
Toole, Briana. 2021. Recent Work in Standpoint Epistemology. *Analysis* 81 (2): 338–350.
Von Neumann, John, and Oskar Morgenstern. 2007. *Theory of Games and Economic Behavior*, 60th Anniversary Edition. Princeton: Princeton University Press.
Williams, Christine. 1992. The Glass Escalator: Hidden Advantages for Men in the 'Female' Professions. *Social Problems* 39: 253–267.
———. 2013. The Glass Escalator, Revisited: Gender Inequality in Neoliberal Times. *Gender & Society* 27 (3): 609–629.

Wingfield, Adia Harvey. 2009. Racializing the Glass Escalator: Reconsidering Men's Experiences with Women's Work. *Gender & Society* 23: 5–26.

Wollstonecraft, Mary. 1792. *A Vindication of the Rights of Woman*. London: Joseph Johnson.

Wylie, Alison. 2012. Feminist Philosophy of Science: Standpoint Matters. *Proceedings and Addresses of the American Philosophical Association* 86 (2): 47–76.

**Open Access**  This chapter is licensed under the terms of the Creative Commons Attribution 4.0 International License (http://creativecommons.org/licenses/by/4.0/), which permits use, sharing, adaptation, distribution and reproduction in any medium or format, as long as you give appropriate credit to the original author(s) and the source, provide a link to the Creative Commons licence and indicate if changes were made.

The images or other third party material in this chapter are included in the chapter's Creative Commons licence, unless indicated otherwise in a credit line to the material. If material is not included in the chapter's Creative Commons licence and your intended use is not permitted by statutory regulation or exceeds the permitted use, you will need to obtain permission directly from the copyright holder.

CHAPTER 7

# Afterword: Man Up/Stand Up

**Abstract** To conclude, we contrast feminist allyship masculinity with a familiar expression of hegemonic masculinity: the exhortation to "man up!" Both have normative force; both capture and convey expectations (patriarchal, feminist, or otherwise) of how men should be. But what differentiates feminist allyship as nontoxic masculinity is the sort of normative direction it gives: not to man up, but to stand up for gender justice from our situated positions and distinctive capacities as men in patriarchal societies.

**Keywords** Normativity • Masculinity • Feminism

A personal confession by way of conclusion: I hated the phrase "man up" for a long time, and to be honest I am still pretty wary of it. What does it mean, exactly, to "punitively invoke the idea of manning up" (Conroy 2018)? Whether said in aggressive, combative, homophobic, misogynistic, or gently paternalistic contexts, the tacit or explicit message is that somebody is not being man enough and needs to fix that straightaway—even as the success conditions for doing so are left unexplained (Allan 2018, 175). Whatever initial force it might have seems inevitably to collapse under the slightest critical interrogation. When "man up" means conforming to toxic masculinity—stifling one's emotions, responding violently to some provocation, speaking with an unearned and unwarranted sense of authority—so much the worse for it. When "man up" means having courage, taking responsibility, fulfilling obligations, and so on (Hemmer 2017), the follow-up question is why such things have been oddly and selectively identified as *masculine* rather than as gender non-specific good human behaviors. Do women man up when they rise to the occasion and fulfill some obligation they would rather skip? Do preschoolers man up when they eat their vegetables? Can a football coach rouse his players to man up, not to play through pain but to practice tackling to avoid helmet-to-helmet contact?

Feminist allyship masculinity does not ask us to man up, but to step up as men, to stand against patriarchal norms, cultures, and institutions in our capacities *as* men. As I hope has become clear, by this I don't mean *as* breadwinners, *as* protectors, or *as* male halves of some biological, mythical, or symbolic duality. Contrary to how the phrase is often used, we will *be men* just as much whether we stifle doubt, command a room, or collaborate with others in contributing to feminist projects. I am reminded of *Man up*'s similarly fraught cousin *Be a man!*—perhaps an even worse candidate for feminist reclamation, not because men cannot be feminists but because of its accompanying assumptions that manhood is something that can be lost and that manhood regained is the solution to what ails us.

If there is a constructive role for "man up" as a reclaimed norm of feminist masculinity, it is if its normativity can be disentangled from the toxic gender essentialism that often accompanies it. Within an exhortation to man up is a normative judgment, not only that the speaker wants us to do such-and-such, but that we should. Some readers may want to give up on normative masculinity altogether, abandon all judgments of how men should act, and leave us to live unencumbered by expectations. But recall Mary Anne Warren's critique of the polyandrogynous ideal where people avail themselves of traditionally masculine and traditionally feminine traits or roles without limit: it is too sweeping to be a viable feminist ideal. Giving up normative masculinity is consistent with men exhibiting the most vicious sorts of human character traits, so long as these traits are no longer tied to evaluative analyses of how men should be. This is why Warren's preferred ideal of feminist androgyny retains a normative dimension, where *virtues* are distributed and enacted among human beings regardless of sex or gender identity (1982, 183). A feminist attempt to reclaim masculinity needs a normative dimension as well, some feminist vision and guidance for what we should do and how we should be.

In doing the work of feminist allyship masculinity, men across a diversity of social locations can contribute to and thereby authentically identify with emancipatory histories and communities. The call to step up in feminist allyship, to stand against cultures and institutions of oppression in a way that takes seriously our social locations as men and their attendant epistemic and practical implications, has normative and hermeneutical power to make sense of our social experiences in a gendered world. Engaging in allyship practices in a patriarchal society is a meaningfully gendered activity: not to be *more* of a man but to perform *better* masculinity, though not what drill sergeants, football coaches, or exacting fathers might have had in mind. We can make feminist masculinity be about standing against patriarchal cultures and institutions in our capacities as men alongside differently positioned others, and in so doing, envision and enact a healthier, revitalizing, and substantively feminist alternative to masculinity as traditionally configured.

## References

Allan, Jonathan. 2018. Masculinity as Cruel Optimism. *NORMA: International Journal for Masculinity Studies* 13 (3–4): 175–190.

Conroy, Michael. 2018. 'Manning Up' Harms Us All. *The Teacher Magazine*, September.

Hemmer, Jeffrey. 2017. *Man Up! The Quest for Masculinity*. St. Louis: Concordia Publishing.

Warren, Mary Anne. 1982. Is Androdyny the Answer to Sexual Stereotyping? In *'Masculinity,' 'Femininity,' and 'Androgyny': A Modern Philosophical Discussion*, ed. Mary Vetterling-Braggin, 170–185. Totowa, NJ: Rowman & Allanheld.

**Open Access** This chapter is licensed under the terms of the Creative Commons Attribution 4.0 International License (http://creativecommons.org/licenses/by/4.0/), which permits use, sharing, adaptation, distribution and reproduction in any medium or format, as long as you give appropriate credit to the original author(s) and the source, provide a link to the Creative Commons licence and indicate if changes were made.

The images or other third party material in this chapter are included in the chapter's Creative Commons licence, unless indicated otherwise in a credit line to the material. If material is not included in the chapter's Creative Commons licence and your intended use is not permitted by statutory regulation or exceeds the permitted use, you will need to obtain permission directly from the copyright holder.

# Index[1]

## A
Accountability, 7, 51, 74, 92, 93, 101, 102
Alcoff, Linda, 6, 61–63, 68, 83
Allies, 66
Ally, 39
Allyship, 4, 63, 65, 67, 71, 75–77, 84, 86, 92, 101
   masculinities, 7, 68, 71, 72, 75, 84, 90
Androgyny, 4, 5, 25, 26, 32, 33, 36, 37, 40, 47, 49, 50, 52, 64, 70, 83, 84, 90, 110

## B
Black men, 87
Brod, Harry, 38, 63, 69
Bystanders, 66, 92, 98, 100

## C
Communities, 62, 63, 70, 77, 86, 89
Community-building, 51
Concept, 1, 3
Connell, R.W., 3, 8, 68

## D
Democratic manhood, 6, 49, 51
Differences, 64, 67, 68, 76, 101
Differentiation, 8, 50, 57, 76, 83
Distinctive, 75
Double consciousness, 62, 68
Double vision, 5, 38
Du Bois, W.E.B., 62, 68

## E
Education, 18, 19, 88
End to manhood, 46

---

[1] Note: Page numbers followed by 'n' refer to notes.

Epistemic, 22, 25, 36, 69, 85, 89, 90
Epistemically, 23
Epistemic injustices, 88, 101, 102
Epistemological, 7
Epistemologies, 88, 90

# F
Female masculinity, 70
Feminine, 23, 24, 32, 33, 84, 88
Femininity, 16, 19, 35, 50, 70
Feminism, 67
  liberal, 16, 20, 33
  minoritarian, 71n2
  radical, 21, 34n2
  trans-inclusive, 54, 68
  visionary, 44, 47, 52, 53
Feminist, 40, 67, 94
  allies, 67, 93
  allyship, 63–70, 83, 91, 96, 101;
    masculinities, 6, 67, 88, 98, 110, 111
  androgyny, 25, 33, 44, 51, 71
  manhood, 83
  masculinities, 4, 6, 43, 44, 47, 51, 57, 63, 64, 75, 77, 85, 90

# H
Halberstam, Jack, 70, 70n1
Hegemonic masculinity, 35, 97, 100, 101
Hegemonic patriarchal masculinity, 44
hooks, bell, 6, 43–45, 50, 53, 64, 65, 83

# I
Ignorance, 88–90, 101
Injustice, 74, 85, 87, 95, 97
Intersecting, 86
Intersectional, 7, 45, 68, 75, 76, 84, 86
  feminism, 87
  feminist, 87
Intersectionality, 9, 66, 75–77, 87

# J
Justice, 33, 44, 48, 51

# K
Katz, Jackson, 73, 97, 99, 100
Kimmel, Michael, 6, 47, 50, 51, 53, 94
Kivel, Paul, 92

# L
Liberal feminism, 16, 20, 33
Liberal feminist, 24
Liberating masculinity, 55, 56
Lorde, Audre, 64, 97, 98

# M
Manhood
  Black, 66, 67, 87
  democratic, 6, 49–51, 56
  feminist, 45, 51, 83
  repudiation of, 5, 36, 54, 68
Masculine, 24, 32, 33, 76
Masculinities, 16, 19, 24, 35, 36, 40, 44, 50, 55, 68, 87, 94
  allyship, 6, 7, 64, 67–72, 74, 75, 77, 83–103, 110, 111
  Black, 66, 67, 87
  female, 10, 70
  feminist, 4, 6, 8–10, 40, 43–48, 50, 51, 53, 54, 57, 61–77, 85, 86, 90, 98, 110, 111
  hegemonic, 35, 36, 97, 100, 101
  liberating, 55–57
  mindful, 3, 6, 37, 54–57
  mythopoetic, 7, 84

normative, 8, 9, 70, 70n1, 72, 76, 85, 110
patriarchal, 6, 7, 9, 26, 36, 43–46, 50, 52–54, 71, 85
reclamations of, 6, 26, 37, 43–57
toxic, 1–5, 8, 10, 26, 32, 40, 51, 54, 68, 83, 85, 96, 109
Master's tools, 8, 97, 98
Master's tools problem, 97, 98, 101
May, Larry, 8, 69
Mill, John Stuart, 4, 20–26, 88
Mindful masculinity, 37, 54, 55
Minoritarian feminism, 71n2
Mythopoetic masculinity, 84
Mythopoetic men, 50
Mythopoetic men's movement, 46

## N
Narayan, Uma, 91–93
Normative, 2, 3, 63, 83, 96
  feminist masculinity, 68
  masculinity, 8, 70, 76
Normativity, 8, 110
Norms, 77, 90

## O
Oppression, 61, 66, 68, 74, 85–87, 90, 93, 97
Oppressive, 89

## P
Partnership, 46, 50
Patriarchal, 22, 35, 69, 75, 90, 94, 98, 99, 101
Patriarchal masculinity, 6, 43, 52, 71
Patriarchy, 44, 45, 68, 73, 76, 86, 89
Plank, Liz, 37, 38, 54, 55
Pride, 69
Privileges, 23, 39, 48, 63, 68, 75–77, 87, 93–101

## R
Racism, 72, 75, 86, 87
Radical feminist, 20, 34
Rational, 5, 17, 20
Rationality, 16, 18, 19
Rational masculinity, 26
Reason, 18
Reclaimed masculinity, 53
Reclaim masculinity, 44
Reclamation of masculinity, 51
Reclamations of masculinity, 26, 46
Refuse to be a man, 4
Refusing manhood, 39
Relational, 56, 63–69, 74
Relationality, 73
Relationally, 64
Relationships, 45, 47
Reparative, 74
Reparative justice, 39
Repudiation of manhood, 5, 36

## S
Standpoint, 7, 69, 89
  theorists, 89
  theory, 91
Sterba, James, 5, 33, 37, 40, 51, 94
Stoltenberg, John, 5, 34, 35, 38, 40, 63

## T
Taylor, Harriet, 4, 21–24
Toxic, 55
Toxic masculinity, 1, 3, 26, 51, 68, 83, 85, 96, 109

Traditional masculinity, 49
Trans-positive feminist theorizing, 54

**U**
Unjust, 36
Unjust meantime, 85
Unjust patriarchal, 39

**V**
Visionary feminism, 52
Visionary feminist, 43, 45

**W**
Warren, Mary Anne, 5, 31, 33, 37, 40, 110
White, 70, 72
White anti-racism, 6
Whiteness, 39, 61–63, 83, 86, 87
Why can't manhood and masculinity be redeemed?, 34
Wollstonecraft, Mary, 4, 16–18, 23, 24, 26, 88
Women's masculinity, 18

The manufacturer's authorised representative in the EU is Springer Nature Customer Service Centre GmbH, Europaplatz 3, 69115 Heidelberg, Germany. If you have any concerns regarding our products, please contact ProductSafety@springernature.com

Printed and bound by CPI Group (UK) Ltd, Croydon, CR0 4YY

25/03/2026

02078179-0008